MEMORIZE THE LATIN MASS!

MEMORIZE THE LATIN MASS!

How to Remember and Treasure Its Rites

Kevin Vost, Psy.D.

⊛*ENROUTE*

ENROUTE

5705 Rhodes Avenue

St. Louis, MO 63109

Contact us at contactus@enroutebooksandmedia.com

Cover design by TJ Burdick

Altar piece image, *Altar with 3 canonical textboards*

by FaceMePLS, via flikr: https://www.flickr.com/pho-

tos/38891071@N00/2068721172/

Image edited by T.J. Burdick.

Library of Congress Control Number: 2018952256

ISBN-13: 978-1-950108-52-7

ISBN-10: 1-950108-52-X

Printed in the United States of America

1 3 5 7 9 10 8 6 4 2

CONTENTS

PREFACE   1

INTRODUCTION   7

PART 1: Mass of the Catechumens   23

PART 2: Mass of the Faithful   51

PART 3: Canon of the Mass   65

PART 4: Consecration Rites   73

PART 5: Communion Rites   87

PART 6: Post-Communion Rites   99

CONCLUSION   107

APPENDIX A   115

APPENDIX B   119

WHEN ONE'S LIFE DEPENDS ON THE MASS

As in all other times of crisis, we relied on our religious backgrounds to give us strength and to help us accept the sacrifice of our monastic existence. I went through the Mass each day in English and Latin, took spiritual communion, and meditated deeply.

Admiral Jeremiah Denton[1]

In early 2015, I was working on a book about the Stoic philosophers. While examining their ongoing modern-day influence, I told the story of James Stockdale, a U.S. Navy naval fighter pilot who was shot from the skies over North Vietnam on September 9, 1965, and would remain a prisoner of the North Vietnamese Communist army for more than seven years. He attributed his success in holding

---

1 Admiral Jeremiah A. Denton, *When Hell Was in Session* (Washington, DC: WorldNetDaily, 1998), 189.

up mentally to repeated bouts of torture and isolation and in giving solace to his fellow American POWs to his previous immersion in the ancient Stoic wisdom of the philosopher Epictetus. Epictetus taught that to maintain emotional tranquility, grow in virtue, and conform our will to God's, it is essential to distinguish between what we can control and what we cannot control. Sometimes what we can control is little beyond our own mental judgments, attitudes, and moral purpose. We must focus our efforts on those things we can control and endure with dignity events that are not up to us. Stockdale strove to control his own moral purpose and state of mind, since so little else was left up to him. He survived the ordeal and later became an admiral and the vice-presidential running mate with Ross Perot in the 1992 presidential elections.

In the midst of writing that book,[2] I received an email from Major Valpiani, a U.S. Air Force officer and experimental test pilot. He had read one of my books on the memory techniques of Sts. Albert the Great and Thomas Aquinas, and he asked me if I could give him suggestions on how to memorize the parts of the Mass. You see, he had found through the Internet that I'd written an article called "Memorize the Mass!" on a now defunct Catholic social media site, and he wondered if I could share it with him. I remembered the article but found that my Word program didn't!

I was unable to track down the article for him, but I told him that I remembered the basics and could share those with him. What in-

---

2 Kevin Vost, *The Porch and the Cross: Ancient Stoic Wisdom for Modern Christian Living* (Kettering, OH: Angelico Press, 2016).

trigued me about his email, however, was the story behind his question.

Major Valpiani had heard a recording of a talk from a man who had mentally repeated the Mass every day to preserve his sanity and sanctity during nearly eight years of confinement, also as a POW in North Vietnam, like Stockdale. That man, Jeremiah Denton, had been Commanding Officer of Attack Squadron Seventy-Five aboard the USS Independence and was shot down on July 18, 1965, two months before James Stockdale. His ordeal as a POW would last nearly eight years. He, like Stockdale, would later become an admiral, and then he became a U.S. senator from Alabama. I responded to the major that I had not heard of Admiral Denton, but I had, coincidentally just written about Admiral Stockdale. In his response he told me that in fact the two were friends! That was news to me. Stockdale had not mentioned Denton in the books I'd read. Admiral Denton's story was clearly one that I had to investigate.

Sure enough, in his book *Hell is in Session*, Denton described how he and Stockdale cooperated in keeping the American POWs alive and in preserving their dignity. He described as well, in the quotation that started this preface, that throughout those years, many of which included solitary confinement and a variety of ongoing tortures, he did indeed go through the Mass each day in his head, both in English and in Latin!

Well, not long after this interchange, a Maryknoll missionary priest came to my parish and told the story of Bishop James Walsh, who was imprisoned in Communist China for nearly twelve years (1958-1970). Though he could not actually celebrate the Mass, the Mass and the Rosary gave him strength throughout his years of imprisonment. Indeed, so great was his love for the Mass that in the bishop's book *Zeal for Your House,* one photo shows him in a hospital bed just after his release, joyfully celebrating the Holy Mass for the first time after so many years, whilst still in his pajamas!

To keep a short preface from becoming long, these stories made it quite clear to me that providing a simple means of "memorizing the Mass," coming to know all of its parts, both backwards and forwards, would well be worth not just another article, but an entire book. Thankfully, Dr. Sebastian Mahfood and Shaun McAfee at En-Route Books agreed.

The story did not end there, however. In November of 2017 I received a gracious email from another reader, this time not from an experimental jet fighter pilot in California, but from a reader in the midwest with another vocation, perhaps less exotic, but also of inestimable value to our nation – that of "a devoted traditional grandmother who wishes to have all her precious grandbabies know and love the Mass" who "believes Dr. Vost's memory method will contribute significantly to that goal." She informed me that she had read some of my books including *Memorize the Mass!* and she asked if it would be feasible to craft a book focusing exclusively on the Traditional Latin Mass to serve as an aid to parents whose children are attending and learning that Mass. I thought this an interesting proposal, and once again, the good people at En Route Books and Media agreed.

After all, when Admiral Denton and Bishop Walsh recited the Mass daily during their years of confinement, it was indeed the Latin Mass they recited. Even when Jeremiah Denton said he recited that Mass *in English*, it was *the English translation of the Traditional Latin Mass*, like those we find in a Latin Mass hymnal, since he was captured in 1965, four years before the time of the *Novus Ordo* Mass was promulgated.

So then, here, in *Memorize the Latin Mass!* we focus entirely on the Traditional Latin Mass[3] with adapted text from *Memorize the Mass!* and a new Appendix on The Last Gospel. Those who have read *Memorize the Mass!* will find much of the information in that book duplicated here. This more slender volume has been prepared for those who want a primer for themselves, their children, grandchildren—and perhaps great grandchildren, to help them come to better know and love the still enduring form of the sacrifice of the Mass that has nourished countless great saints for the vast majority of the history of the Catholic Church. Further, as much as the lives of Admiral Denton and Bishop Walsh depended on the Mass under such extreme crises, in a way, *all our lives depend upon it, most particularly our eternal lives.*

The goal then of this book is to help you, reader, through the implementation of specialized memory methods recommended and employed by Saints Albert the Great and Thomas Aquinas, to more fully and deeply experience all of the blessings and graces of the Holy Sacrifice of the Mass in this life and the next, by writing the Holy Sacrifice of the Mass on the tablet of your heart.

---

3 Also known as the Tridentine Mass of the council of Trent and Pope Pius V, the Gregorian Rite, the *usus antiquior*, *vetus ordo*, and the Extraordinary Form of the Roman Rite.

The Catholic Art of Memory Meets the Holy Sacrifice of the Mass

"The Sacrifice (of the Mass) is celebrated with many solemn rites and ceremonies, none of which should be deemed useless or superfluous. On the contrary, all of them tend to display the majesty of this august Sacrifice, and to excite the faithful when beholding these saving mysteries, to contemplate the divine things which lie concealed in the Eucharistic Sacrifice."

Catechism of the Council of Trent[1]

"Nothing that you have seen or heard is useful, however, unless you deposit what you should see and hear in the treasury of your memory."

St. Jerome[2]

---

1 John A McHugh, O.P, & Charles J. Callan, OP, trans. *Catechism of the Council of Trent for Parish Priests* (Rockford, IL :TAN Books, 1982), 276.

2 Cited in Mary Carruthers, *The Book of Memory: A Study of Memory in Medieval Culture* (Cambridge: Cambridge University Press, 1990), 18.

The Mass is the heart of Catholic life, and the Eucharist is that heart's flesh and blood, the Body, Blood, Soul and Divinity of our Savior Jesus Christ. Christ initiated the Eucharist for us nearly two thousand years ago, and the Church has been greatly blessed by it and by the rites of the Holy Sacrifice that so quickly grew around it to perfect it is as the Church's ultimate act of worship.

The Holy Sacrifice of the Mass has four main ends or goals of adoration, thanksgiving, reparation, and prayer. The first end of the Mass is to honor and glorify God. The second end is to give Him thanks, to show gratitude for the countless benefits he has bestowed upon us, including our very existence. Indeed, the word Eucharist itself comes from the Greek ευχαριστα, meaning thankfulness. The third end is to obtain remission of the many venial sins we have made against God, atoning for our petty, ungrateful thoughts, desires, words, and deeds. The fourth end is to obtain earthly and eternal benefits and graces for ourselves and others through petitionary prayer.

As great as these ends are, the Mass is also a foretaste of heaven on earth and, indeed, it brings Christ Himself from heaven right into our midst in his sacramental, Eucharistic presence. Truly, there is nothing else to compare with the treasure we have in the likes of the Holy Mass.

Like the Back of Your Hand

Many of us adult Catholics have attended Mass for decades and have experienced it hundreds, if not thousands, of times. Surely we've seen and held a simple penny countless times, too, yet how many of us could accurately draw its details from memory? For that matter, could you right now, draw from memory the lines of your own palms, or even the veins on the back of your hands? After all, a common idiom indicating that someone has mastered some subject is to say that he knows it "like the back of his hand." Yet, how well do we really know the backs of our own hands, despite the countless times we have seen them? Even more so, regardless of how many Masses we've attended, how well do we really know the Mass? How well do we know the histories of the various prayers, their origins in the Bible and in Church Tradition, the reasons for our various gestures and postures, not to mention the origin and order of the various parts or rites of the Mass?

Well, the end or goal of this book is to assist you in better attaining all the ends of the Mass, to better praise God, to more sincerely repent of our sins, to better give Him thanks, and to ever more devoutly present our petitions before him, by a far greater internal participation in the Holy Sacrifice Christ gave us. The text and illustrations have been structured in such a way that, if you read slowly and carefully, look at the pictures, and follow the detailed step-by-step instructions, by the time you finish, you will be able to name and remember all 42 parts of the Traditional Latin Mass. This beautiful Mass has endured with only minor gradual changes over nearly two millennia. You will remember all the rites, including their Latin names, from the Mass of the Catechumens, to the Mass of the Faithful, the Canon of the Mass, the rites of the Consecration, and Communion, all way to the Post-Communion rites including the Last Gospel. These, too, you will come to know literally forward and backward, from 1 to 42 and from 42 to back to 1. Now talk about knowing something *better than* the back of your hand!

The Catholic Art of Memory

Plain as day within the written works of two of the best known and greatest Catholic Doctors of the Church, Saint Albert the Great and Saint Thomas Aquinas, lies what we might call a "Catholic Art of Memory," and yet most of our modern world seems to have forgotten it! During the thirteenth century in their work as philosophers, theologians, and university professors, Sts. Albert and Thomas carefully examined, explained, and endorsed an ancient system of memory improvement, invented, it was said, by the Greek poet Simonides of Ceos (556-468 BC), and passed on to the Latin West primarily through the works of Marcus Tullius Cicero (107-43 BC). It became known in the West as "the method of loci" (*loci* being the Latin plural for locations.) Not only did Albert and Thomas expound upon and endorse these memory methods, they integrated or synthesized the ancient literature on *memory improvement* with Aristotle's writings on *the nature of human memory*, showing not only that the memory methods work, but shedding light on why they are so effective.

It is not entirely surprising, however, that Sts. Albert and Thomas's methods were all but forgotten. One event that likely played a large role was Gutenberg's invention of the printing press around the year 1440, one-hundred and sixty years after St. Albert's death.

With easy access to printed materials, a powerful memory perhaps no longer seemed so essential. It also did not help that many of Albert's writings have not been translated into vernacular languages from the Latin, and even though St. Thomas's *Summa Theologica* has been widely translated and circulated throughout the centuries, it is a book of over three thousand pages, and his article on the memory method takes up only about one page, almost in the very middle![3]

It is there in his question entitled "Whether Memory is a Part of Prudence?" that Thomas explains and recommends the method in a way that may not be entirely clear if one has not been exposed, as he and his readers were, to the ancient art of "artificial" (man-made) memory.[4] St. Thomas had a tremendous gift for penetrating into the heart of any matter that came under the laser-like light of his lofty intellect. Here is how he summarized the four main features of that ancient art of memory:

There are four things whereby a man perfects his memory.

First, when a man wishes to remember a thing, he should take *some suitable yet unwonted illustration of it,* since the unwonted strikes us more, and so makes a greater and stronger impression on the mind.

---

3 *Summa Theologica*, II-II, Q. 49, art.1. Thomas also considers "Whether Memory is in the Intellectual Soul? in I, Q 79. A. 6. His answer, like St. Augustine's before him (354-430), was yes.

4 I have provided more extensive discussions of St. Thomas's role in the art of memory in *Memorize the Faith!* (Sophia Institute Press, 2006), and of St. Albert's role in *Memorize the Reasons!* (Catholic Answers Press, 2013). I'll provide just a very terse summary here, but enough for our purposes.

Secondly, whatever a man wishes to retain in his memory he must carefully consider to *put in order*, so that he may pass easily from one memory to another.

Thirdly, we must be *anxious and earnest* about the things we wish to remember, because the more a thing is impressed on the mind, the less it is liable to slip out of it.

Fourthly, we should *often reflect* on the things we wish to re-member... Wherefore when we reflect on a thing frequently, we quickly call it to mind, through passing from one thing to another by a kind of natural order" (II-II, Q. 49, art. 1, numbers and emphasis added.)

So, in a nutshell that will soon mature into the full-grown oak of artificial memory, Thomas recommends that we form mental *images,* place them in a certain *order, concentrate* on them intently, and *rehearse* or *repeat* them often. Seven hundred years and at least as many scientific studies later, any honest modern memory training expert will have to admit that St. Thomas Aquinas got it right!

We will see very clearly how those four elements of images, order, concentration, and repetition will enable us to memorize the parts of the Mass because *the heart of this book will include a step-by-step, fully guided tutorial in the use and the mastery of this memory system as applied to the Latin Mass.*

Sometimes Silly Images: Always Sacred Rites

One thing to bear in mind as we apply this memory method to the parts of the Holy Mass is that while the memory images we use will oftentimes seen odd, humorous, and grossly exaggerated, the Rites of the Mass that they hold in mind for us are always holy and sacred. We will keep at the forefronts of our minds that as the map is not the territory, our sometimes silly images are not the always sacred rites they hold in mind for us.

Admiral Denton, while prisoner in North Vietnam, made headlines around the world when during a film produced by his Communist captors for their propaganda purposes, he stealthily revealed to the world that the POWs were indeed being tortured, by using his eyes to blink out the word "torture" in Morse code! So crafty too were he and his men that when transported in vehicles together while forbidden to talk, they communicated to each other by tapping on their neighbor's knees with their knees, again, in Morse code!

In a somewhat similar way, the memory images we will use are but a code for the deep truths they will serve to represent and call to mind. Further, the images need to be striking because that is how our memory works. Saint Thomas himself states that even spiritual ideas are best remembered through images of physical things "because human memory has a greater hold on sensible objects." Further, in referring to using "unwonted" illustrations, Thomas uses the Latin word *miramur* to describe these images – things at which we marvel or wonder. St. Albert, echoing the oldest extant memory improvement treatise, the *ad Herennium,* long attributed to Cicero, explicitly advised that these memory images be made "as striking as possible," to picture them "doing something" and having "exceptional beauty or ugliness."[5]

We are bombarded everyday with so many countless impressions, that we naturally remember best what is most unusual and striking. Those are the kinds of events that we might say impress our memories, making a firm impression upon them. Of course Christ Himself was well aware of the use of colorful stories and images in helping learn spiritual lessons. He taught, after all, in parables and was no stranger at all to colorful phrases from a camel passing through the eye of a needle to the straining out a gnat and the swallowing of a camel (Matt. 19:24; 23:24)!

So, these images, though unusual and light-hearted, will present us with no "Clown Mass" or anything of the sort. They do nothing to counter the sacredness of the rites of the Mass themselves. Further, I assure you that after you have thoroughly mastered the parts of the Mass with this method, you will find over time that you'll know the parts in order even without the images. Our goal, after all, is to write the Mass on the tablets of our hearts.

The Holy Sacrifice of the Mass

The Traditional Latin Mass is a most beautiful thing, remembered

---

5 From *De Bono* (On the Good), cited in Mary Carruthers, *The Book of Memory,* 275.

and cherished by many priests, religious, and lay persons who have grown with it, as well as by those who have discovered its treasures later in life. It can also be a bit daunting though for those of us who grew up under the Ordinary Form. I attended the Latin Mass during my own childhood years but have only the vaguest memories, since the New Order Mass replaced it in my dioceses when I was only about nine years old. In rediscovering the Latin Mass in my adult years, I have seen that it can prove difficult to follow, even when guided by a Missal, partly because so much of the Mass, especially the Low Mass I've usually attended, is carried out in a beautiful, reverent silence.

Growing numbers of Catholics across the United States are blessed with the opportunity to glorify God through our participation in the Latin Mass.[6] In my own small city of Springfield in Central, Illinois, we were blessed by our bishops' invitation to three priests, Canons of St. John Cantius, to come to town down from Chicago and administer a combined parish with two churches. They now offer the Latin Mass daily. If you are not aware of one in your area, you might consider checking the Internet for the nearest Latin Mass to attend at least occasionally, even if it might still be some distance away.

Hopefully, the memory exercises and commentary in this book

---

6 Peter Kwasnieswki, in *Noble Beauty, Transcendent Holiness: Why the Modern Age Needs the Mass of Ages* (Kettering, OH: Angelico Press, 2017) cites a source reporting that while in 1998 Latin Mass was celebrated at about only 20 places in the entire United States, by 2013 the number had reached nearly 500. The Coalition is Support of *Ecclesia Dei* in Chicago lists the locations and times of Latin Masses throughout the U.S. and Canada. See http://www.ecclesiadei.org/masses.cfm.

will help open up the Latin Mass to those who are new to it, and to those who know it well, but seek to know and love it even better. Though it is not necessary, I would encourage readers who are not fluent in the rites of the Latin Mass to obtain and follow along as well with a Latin-English Booklet Missal.[7] Further, I will note again, that in laying out 42 parts, I followed the headings in Dom Prosper Gueranger, O.S.B.'s *Explanation of the Holy Mass.* That book may also be a valuable resource in helping you to come to know and love each of the rites of the Latin Mass, in order. Note well that there are some distinctions between the more complex and elaborate "High Mass" and the more common, routine, and relatively silent read Mass or "Low Mass."[8] Most of the rites we will focus on appear in the Low Mass, though I times I will note the exceptions.

To come to better know and love the Holy Mass is indeed the end

---

7 A simple and beautiful one I use and that is commonly used in my city and which I have relied on both at Latin Mass and within the pages of this book is the *Latin-English Booklet Missal For Praying the Traditional Latin Mass: Commemorative Edition in Thanksgiving for Summorum Pontificum* (Chicago: Coalition in Support of *Ecclesia Dei*, 2015). I have found its illustrations of priest and server and comments on the left and right hand pages are invaluable aids in keeping one's place in the Mass. It uses the Mass of the Holy Trinity as an example, since it was the most frequently used Sunday Mass in the traditional liturgical calendar. An online guide to the rites of the Tridentine Mass with English translations can be found at https://www.catholicamericanthinker.com/Traditional-Latin-Tridentine-Mass.html.

8 Different terms and variations of these Masses include the *Missa Solemnis* (Solemn High Mass), *Missa Cantata* (Sung High Mass), *Missa Lecta* (Read Low Mass), and *Missa Privata* (Low Mass). These vary in features including the number of candles on the altar, use of incense, singing, and whether or not the presiding priest has clerical assistants.

or goal of this book, and the memory methods are but the means. The Traditional Mass is a most beautiful thing that has developed gradually over the course of nearly two millennia. As I guide you through the memory method tutorials in each chapter of this book, please bear in mind that the numerical ordering system I use is to some extent arbitrary. The memory method requires a numbering system to lock things in their exact order (as you'll see it does so well), but the arbitrariness lies in the fact that you will find 42 parts for the Traditional Latin Mass.[9] I use 42 parts because, at first unable to find a comparably numbered missal for the Tridentine Mass, I simply followed the helpful section headings in Dom Prosper Gueranger, O.S.B.'s *Explanation of the Holy Mass.*[10]

As you will come to see, each of those "parts" may include a series of gestures and more than one prayer, or prayers with more than one part.[11] Further, I will note that true mastery of all of the holy rites of the Mass is truly the province only of thoroughly trained and

---

9 Again, please note I will use the terms Traditional Latin Mass or Tridentine Mass interchangeably to the Mass Pope St. Pius V promulgated in 1570 and which last appeared in a 1962 edition during the pontificate of Pope St. John XXIII.

10 *Explanation of the Prayers and Ceremonies of the Holy Mass: Taken From Notes Made at the Conferences of Dom Prosper Gueranger, Abbot of Solesmes* (Fitzwilliam, NH: Loreto Publications, 2007).

11 I have since obtained the *Daily Missal and Liturgical Manual for the Roman Missal and Breviary, 1962* (Baronius Press, 2014) and it does contain a numbered sequence of the Ordinary of the Mass on pages 898-899. They have numbered 36 parts, though five of those parts have lettered subparts that would add another 14 parts to a memory tour. I think you will find that our 42 parts parallel those pretty closely and lead to a satisfactory mastery of the parts of the Latin Mass.

ordained priest. There is so much to the Mass that I can barely scratch the surface here, but it is a surface so worth the scratching. My expert role here is not of course as priest or as theologian, but as a master of memory method who relies for his content on saints and theologians faithfully aligned with the glorious Magisterium of the Holy Catholic Church. Be aware too, that I am unable to describe every rite and prayer in the Latin Mass. The best method to learn and treasure the Latin Mass as thoroughly as possible is attend it frequently and read widely about it.

Memoria Verborum/Memoria Rerum

As you complete the memory tour of this book for the first time, you will by no means master all of the words of each of the prayers, unless you already knew them. Even the ancient Roman memory masters distinguished between what they called *memoria verborum* (memory for words) and *memoria rerum* (memory for things). The ancient art of memory we are applying here is *not* best suited for memory for words, that is, word-for-word rote memorization of the exact wording or texts or prayers. It may be used to assist in such verbatim memorization if difficulties arise in a particular part of a particular prayer, but its main function lies within the realm of *memoria rerum,* memory for things, and those "things" we will remember are the most important "things" in the world: the names, sequence, and significance of the holy rites of the Mass. Through weekly (ideally daily), attendance at Mass, those prayers, too, if not yet memorized will work their way as well into the treasuries of your memory if you pay close *attention* to them and *repeat* them again and again and again.[12]

I will note as well that while this book may be read on its own and used as an aide for Mass, if you are not already well-versed in the Latin Mass at the start, you would do very well to use this book to supplement a formal missal while you read it at home and while actually present at Mass. If the Missal is your personal copy and is not already numbered, it may be of help to neatly add the numbers in pencil at the start of the appropriate parts in your missal. (I found this a huge help in grasping, retaining, and better appreciating the Traditional Latin Mass as an adult because, though I was taken to Latin Mass as a child, I was not blessed to attend one again until my late 40s!) If all goes as planned, these methods will help your missal come alive for you, resonating with more meaning and helping you further write in your heart the holy treasures of the Holy Mass.

I would hope, too, that if you are helping your child learn to know and love the Latin Mass, you will find this book a useful aid to you. Many readers of my other memory books have told me they and their children have found the use of these memory methods not only effective, but *fun*. *The memory exercises in this book can be used with parents*

---

12 Recall, if you will, that *concentration* and *repetition* are themselves two of the four things that, according to St. Thomas, perfect the human memory. As for the specialized methods of *images* and *order* you will find in the pages ahead, while they too still require focused concentration and repeated efforts, I think you will find them effective, and as some readers of my previous memory books have noted, even *fun* as well, for it seems that our modern-day neglected memory muscles actually relish a challenging workout!

and children- indeed, they may be practiced aloud by entire families, and I hope and pray that your family will be one of them!

Let's forge on ahead then and actually begin to memorize the Mass as if our very lives depended on it -- because they do. Without further ado, let us "go up to the altar" to share in the great mystery of the greatest sacrifice of all.

Holy Mass is the sun of all spiritual exercises, the mainspring of devotion, the soul of piety, the fire of divine charity, the abyss of divine mercy and a precious means whereby God confers upon us His graces.

St. Francis de Sales, Introduction to a Devout Life[13]

Treasures, however great and precious, are never appreciated until examined, counted over, and summed up. Hence it is, dear reader, that by many there is formed no due estimate of the holy and awful sacrifice of the Mass. Though the greatest treasure which glories and enriches the Church of God, it is still a hidden treasure, and known to few. Ah, if this jewel of paradise were but known, who would not give up all things to obtain it!

St. Leonard of Port Maurice[14]

There is no contradiction between the two editions of the Roman Missal. In the history of the liturgy there is growth and progress, but no rupture. What earlier generations held as sacred, remains sacred and great for us too, and it cannot all of a sudden by entirely forbidden or even considered harmful. It behooves all of us to preserve the riches which have developed in the Church's faith and prayer, and to give them their proper place.

---

13 Cited in Fr. Martin von Cochem, *The Incredible Catholic Mass* (Charlotte, NC: TAN Books, 2012), p. 16.

14 St. Leonard of Port Maurice, *The Hidden Treasure: Holy Mass* (Rockford, IL: TAN Books, 1980), 17.

It has been clearly demonstrated that young persons too have discovered this liturgical form, felt its attraction and found in it a form of encounter with the Mystery of the Most Holy Eucharist particularly suited to them.

Pope Benedict XVI[15]

---

15 Pope Benedict XVI, *Summorum Pontificum,* Letter to the Bishops, July 7, 2007.

— PART 1 —

MASS OF THE CATECHUMENS

*[I]t is the business of the wise man to order. The reason for this is that wisdom
is the most powerful perfection of reason whose characteristic is to know order...
Now a twofold order is found in things. One kind is that of parts of a totality,
that is, a group, among themselves, as the parts of a house are mutually ordered
to each other. The second order is that of things to an end. This order is of
greater importance than the first.*

St. Thomas Aquinas[1]

"As for me and my household, we will serve the LORD."

Joshua 24:15

---

1 St. Thomas Aquinas, *Commentary on Aristotle's Nichomachean Ethics* (Notre
Dame: Dumb Ox Books, 1993), 1.

Welcome (Back) to the House of Memory!

I include the "back" in parenthesis for those who have already been guests to my memory house within the pages of *Memorize the Faith!* or *Memorize the Mass!* We're delighted to have you over once more to see all the new and wonderful things that now lie within these walls.[2] This house houses the holy rites of the Traditional Latin Mass. Of course, first time guests to this house are gladly and equally welcomed. You need not at all have been here before, for we'll happily guide you through every part of every room, never once leaving your side. And as we begin we will keep our end clearly in mind that the parts of this memory house will help you recall the order and meaning of the parts of the holy Mass.

Before we begin our memory tour, I invite you to turn your powers of concentration and imagination as high as they will go, since, after all, we are going to try to remember the noblest and highest sacrificial prayer and liturgical work of the Holy Catholic Church.

Imagine, if you will, that you have arrived at my house, a rather sprawling ranch-style home, nestled beneath the towering leafy canopies of old maples and oaks.

You knock on the front door (location 1), since there is no electric doorbell, and to your surprise you are greeted by old *King David* himself. You can tell by the crown on his head and the slingshot attached to his belt. He blesses you with the *Sign of the Cross*,

---

2 Again, readers are advised that these 42 parts, images, and the majority of accompanying text were provided in the second part of *Memorize the Mass!*

and then, oddly enough, he asks you to judge him, bellowing out: *"Adjudicate me!"*

Moving inside to our familiar door mat (2) you spy an even stranger scene. A *convict* (you can tell by his black and white striped jumpsuit – or orange, if you prefer) is fitting a top hat on Winnie the Pooh's donkey friend Eeyore. (Odd indeed, but you'll soon see the reason behind the madness.) Looking back out through the glass panel next to the door (3), you notice that the front yard has been completely enveloped in a dense cloud of incense. You see it coming in through the crack beneath the front door and you find its aroma is absolutely heavenly. In the picture on the wall next to the door (also known as location 4), you see depicted an old car with a big sign underneath it that says *"Made in Detroit,"* except that the "Made" and the "D" in Detroit have all but faded away over time.

There is a locked gun rack on the right wall[3] (location 5) and as you glance at it you swear you could hear striking strains of familiar symphonic music, of Richard Wagner in fact, for being replaced there are not rifles, but swords and axes, and they're being replaced by sturdy, blonde warrior women! You are struck by the wings on their back. These are no ordinary women, but in fact are the fabled Valkyries.[4]

---

3 A remnant of its first use in *Memorize the Faith!* to remind readers of the Fifth Commandment, "Thou shalt not kill."

4 In ancient Norse mythology, these winged warriors roamed the fields of battle, deciding who would live or die, and carried the souls of the dead to Valhalla, the Viking warrior heaven of sorts. Perhaps Richard Wagner's most famous piece of music is his "Ride of the Valkyries." (Check it out online if you are not familiar.)

(Why are Valkyries in this foyer of the Holy Mass? Good question. That is just the kind of thing we explain later in this chapter.)

Moving on now to the center of the foyer (location 6) who should be standing there, but that famous singer named *Gloria*! (Not familiar with Gloria Gaynor or perhaps Gloria Estefan? No problem, place here any person you know who's named Gloria. Don't know any Glorias? Still no problem, just plant a U. S. flag there – aka, "Old Glory.")

Now, let's pause for just a bit and see if we can recall where we've been and what we've seen before we continue our memory tour. Do you recall King David saying *"Adjudicate me!"* at the front door (location 1), the con fitting *Eeyore* at the doormat (2), the cloud of incense in the front yard seen through the glass panel next to the door (3), the car made in *Detroit* up on the wall (4), the *Valkyries* at the gun rack (5) and Gloria in the center of the foyer (6) ? Sure you do! (At last I hope so, if not, please repeat them another time or two.)

Pressing on and looking overhead at the chandelier (location 7) you see suspended upon it one of those church collection baskets on a stick. You can see that sticking out from the basket, however, are not dollar bills, *but prayers written on slips of paper.*

Now we turn our attention to location 8, a mirror hanging on the foyer's other wall, opposite the gun rack (location 5) that featured those *Valkyries* chanting the *Kyrie*. The mirror contains a disconcerting site. A *letter* is inside the mirror and on it sits a *pistol* emblazoned with a large letter *"E."* Beneath the mirror sits the little cushioned bench (9), and upon that bench sits a young *graduate* you know by the name of *Al*, cap and gown and all. The next thing you know, though,

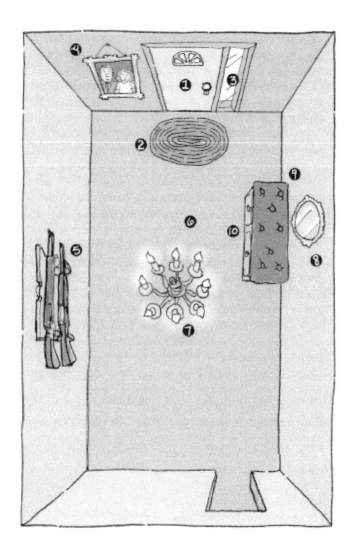

he stands up and starts to climb some stairs that you had not realized were there. In the drawer in the bench (10) you see an even stranger sight, for there is *Al* again, this time with his friend Lulu. (How do we know she's named *Lulu*? Well, it says it on her shirt!) Within that little drawer, they are having a grand old time circling around a tiny toy train track.

Moving from the foyer to the center of the living room (11), you notice a stream of gold objects cascading from the ceiling and forming a glowing and glittering pile on the floor. Upon closer inspection you see that the golden, coin-like discs are decorative *sequins*. Now you spy through the picture window (12) into the back yard. Here you see a young street corner newsboy from days gone by, a satchel around his neck full of newspapers, holding one in his hand. Our newsboy truly captures your attention when he climbs to the top of a tree, proclaiming to all, *"Good news! Good news! Come and get it!"* Finally, you are relieved to see him safely climb down, and your gaze returns to the living room sofa (13). There sit three unusual women in ancient Greek attire. They *profess* that they are three fabled fates as they all sit there spinning thread. Indeed, they then all stand up and tell the host that they are *"Professional Fates."* Here sit then those three professional fates arranged in your opinion into a very nice scene.

And so ends the mnemonic tour of this chapter. Please rehearse a bit and see if you can reel them off: (1) King David saying *"Adjudicate me!"*, (2) the con fitting Eyeore (3), incense, (4) car made in Detroit, (5) Valkyries, (6) Gloria, (7) collection basket (8) letter with pistol with

"E" (9) graduate Al, (10) Al and Lulu on the track, (11) sequins, (12) "Good News!" boy, and (13) professional fates in nice scene.

Second Rehearse, Reverse of the First

Better yet, can you say them all backwards? Practicing with these locations and images in their reverse order from 13 back to 1, and in random order, recalling what was found at location 5 or 9 or 2, etc., can help you attain total memory mastery of the rites of the Latin Mass!

Further, know that once you have memorized this set of locations in their exact order, you can use them over and over again like a mental notepad to remember just about anything you'd like! Indeed, I just discovered this morning (11/28/2017) that there are still some university professors around today who know and promote the power of precisely the same memory methods we are using in this book. To my great delight, I found that my earlier memory book, *Memorize the Faith!* was listed as a reference in a report of an empirical study in a journal of economics and finance, of all places![5]

Getting back now from the things of the world to the things of heaven, let's take a peek at what *we've* memorized, before we spell out

---

5 M. Shaughnessy and Mary L. White, *Making Macro Memorable: The Method of Loci Mnemonic Technique in the Economics Classroom, Journal of Economics and Finance Education*, vol. 11, no. 2, Winter 2012, 131-141. Among their conclusions: "An advantage of the method of loci technique is its applicability to any discipline, and students who discover the technique in an economics course likely will find it useful in any other course that requires some amount of memorization," to which I say, "Amen."

all that it means. (You can also use this table for additional practice if you don't have them all memorized yet.)

LOCATION	*IMAGE*	PART OF MASS
1. Front Door	*King David signs cross, says, "Adjudicate me."*	Judica Me
2. Door mat	*Con fits Eeyore*	Confiteor
3. Glass panel next to door	*Cloud of incense*	Incensing the Altar
4. Picture on wall	*Car made in Detroit, faded D*	Introit
5. Gun rack	*Valkyries*	Kyrie
6. Center of foyer	*Singer or friend named Gloria (or "Old Glory")*	Gloria
7. Chandelier	*Collection basket full of prayers*	Collect
8. Mirror	*Pistol with E rests on letter*	Epistle
9. Bench	*Graduate named Al goes up stairs*	Gradual
10. Drawer	*Al and Lulu on train track*	Alleluia or Tract
11. Center of living room	*Giant golden sequins trickle down*	Sequence
12. Picture window	*Newsboy proclaims "Good news!"*	Gospel
13. Sofa	*Fates in nice scene*	Credo (Profession of Faith/ Nicene Creed)

1. Judica Me

As we approached the front door (1) for the second time, surely you'll recall that King David himself greeted us and asked us to judge him, calling out to us, "Adjudicate me!" This image cannot fail to bring to mind the first part of the Latin Mass known as the *Judica Me*.[6] This first rite takes place right after the priest genuflects before the Altar and declares the sign of the cross in Latin: *"In nomine Patris, +*[7] *et Filii, et Spiritus Sancti. Amen."* Then he says, *"Introibo ad altare Dei,"* to which the server responds, *"Ad Deum qui laetificat juventutem meam."*

The first words of the *Judica Me* are, as you may have guessed, well, "Judica me", as in *"Judge me,"* and further, "Judge me, O God, and distinguish my cause from the nation that is not holy; deliver me from the unjust and deceitful man." These words are based on Psalm 42,[8] largely because of the words that the priest has already prayed and which the server will now pray once again – *"Introibo ad altare Dei,"* "I will go in unto the

---

6 Before High Masses the right of *Asperges,* or sprinkling with holy water, is first performed. Here, in the rite of blessing and sprinkling of holy water, the priest sprinkles the altar, any attendant clergy, and the congregration with holy water using an *aspergillum* (a sacrament instrument of metal with holes at the end that is a literal holy water sprinkler).The rite and the instrument derive their name and meaning from Psalm 50:9 in the Latin Vulgate*, "Asperges me hyssopo et mundabor; lavabis me et super nivem dealbabor"*: "Cleanse me with hyssop, that I may be pure; wash me, and I will be whiter than snow" (Ps 51:7). That verse also begins the prayers of this rite.

7 This symbol represents the many times throughout the Mass when the priest makes the sign of the cross.

8 Psalm 42 in the Latin Vulgate is Psalm 43 in the versions including the New American Bible and the Revised Standard Version. Verse four refers to going to the altar of God, which gave the young psalmist David exceeding joy.

' The priest's words, *"Emitte lucem tuam, et veritatem tuam,"*
hy light and Thy truth," also echo the Psalm, and the serv-
er's response includes the words, *"Ad Deum qui laetificat juventutem meam,"*
"unto God, Who giveth joy to my youth," again echoing the words of
David. The priest also declares, *"Gloria Patri, et Filio, et Spiritui Sancto,"* to
which the server responds, *"Sicut erat in prinicipio et nunc, et semper, et in saecula saeculorum. Amen."* These are the words familiar to us in the "Glory Be":
"Glory be to the Father, and to the Son, and to the Holy Spirit. As it was
in the beginning, is now, and ever shall be, world without end. Amen."

Dom Gueranger reports that the *Judica Me* was not in ancient mis-
sals, but its usage was established by Saint Pope Pius V in 1568. We
kneel during this holy dialogue between the priest and the server.
What a beautiful way to open the Mass, as the priest prepares to ascend the altar, re-presenting the sacrifice Christ offered us on the altar
of Mount Calvary to bring to us the prospect of exceeding joy and
everlasting life. Have we prepared our hearts and minds to ascend
that altar with him?

2. Confiteor

At our entrance mat, we saw that odd scene of a prison convict
fitting a hat on the head of the fictional donkey Eeyore. Silly as it may
seem, the con fitting Eeyore is a pretty straightforward reminder of
the sounds of the Latin word Confiteor. But what does it mean in the
context of the holy sacrifice of the Mass? *"Confiteor Deo Omnipotenti,"*
"I confess to Almighty God," are the words that open this prayer that

may date back to the 8th century. (If you would care to lock in the meaning of confession with the image for the *Confiteor*, I suggest you simply also imagine the "con" fitting Eeyore confessing his crime as he fits him.)

The *Confiteor* in the Latin Mass confesses sins not only to God and to our brothers and sisters, but to the Blessed Virgin, Mary, Michael the Archangel, blessed John the Baptist, to Sts. Peter and Paul and all the Saints, as well, seeking their saintly intercession.

The *Confiteor* also includes the words *"mea culpa,"* "through my fault," three times, while the priest strikes his breast three times, like the tax collector who "beat his breast and prayed, 'O God, be merciful, to me, a sinner'" (Luke 18:13).

The priest then gives the absolution in words that begin, *"Misereatur vestri omnipotens Deus, et dismissis peccatis vestris, perducat vos ad vitam aeternam,"* "May Almighty God have mercy upon you, forgive you your sins, and bring you to life everlasting." The server responds, "Amen."

Next, the priest asks for God's pardon, absolution, and remission of sins for all of us in the first person plural. *Indulgentiam,* + *absolutionem, et remissionem peccatorum, nostrorum tribuat nobis omnipotens et misercors Dominus,* "May the Almighty and merciful God grant us pardon, absolution, and remission of our sins." We all make the sign of the cross as the priest intones the absolution, and the server responds, Amen.

After additional prayers, the priest ascends the altar (and incenses it at High Mass), then moves to the Epistle side to the right of the altar, and begins the next rite of the *Introit*,[9] the formal beginning of the sacrifice of the Mass. Within the priest's remaining prayers, the last words before the Introit are *Dominus Vobiscum*, "The Lord be with you," to which the server responds, *Et cum spiritu tuo*, "And with your spirit." Fr. James W. Jackson, FSSP, building on insights from St. Peter Damien, notes that *Dominus vobiscum* is repeated a total of nine times, now, after the Mass is completed with praying the Last Gospel, and seven times within the Mass itself.[10] The words come from Scripture, repeating a greeting in Ruth 2:4, and they are prayed seven times during the Mass, so that those attending will receive each one of the seven gifts of the Holy Spirit needed to fully participate in the Mass.[11]

The servers' multiple responses of "Amen" through the Mass hark back to the worship of the ancient Hebrews, for it is the Hebrew word for "truth" or "certainty," and has been used by Christians for millennia in Mass as a powerful affirmation meaning, "truly," "verily," or "so be it!" We should hear it or say it not as two mindless syllables we've uttered countless times, but mindfully, joyfully, and with gusto and conviction. This is but one of many "Amens" uttered in Mass, and for centuries it has been among the most notable hallmarks of

9 Though it was omitted from the 1962 missal, in the Tridentine Mass the server also recites the *Confiteor* in the name of the communicants during the Communion rites after the priest has drank the blood of Christ from the cup. The priest responds with the same *Misereatur* and *Indulgentiam* prayers cited above.

10 Rev. James W. Jackson, FSSP, *Nothing Superfluous: An Explanation of the Symbolism of the Rite of St. Gregory the Great* (Lincoln, NE: Rebush, 2016).

11 The seven gifts of the Holy Spiritare wisdom, understanding, counsel, fortitude, knowledge, piety, and fear of the Lord. (See Isaiah 11:1-3.)

Christian worship. Indeed, in one of the ancient lives of St. Patrick, apostle to the Irish, a 5th century Druid priest forewarns the pagan King Laeghaire Mac Neill of a prophetic vision he's had of a new faith that would arrive and live forever in Erin (i.e., Ireland), describing it like this:

> A *Tailecend* (i.e., Patrick) shall come across the stormy sea.
> His garment head-pierced, his staff head-bent,
> His *mias* (i.e., altar) in the east of his house;
> His people all shall answer, Amen, amen.[12]

When we or the servers assent with "Amens," perhaps we can reflect from time to time that we are joined the chorus of the countless "Amens" across time and across nations, recited in every accent imaginable to affirm that great new faith in the Holy Trinity that St. Patrick and multitudes of great saints like him have gone to such great costs to spread unto the ends of the earth, indeed all the way to our very own church!

3. Incensing the Altar

As we looked out the glass panel (3) into the front yard, we saw the air was filled with a cloud of incense. Indeed, it spilled in to us under the front door with the most heavenly aroma. This image represents the incensing of the altar that the priest performs at this point

---

12 Rev. James O'Leary, DD, ed., *The Most Ancient Lives of St. Patrick* (Homer Glen, IL: St. Augustine Academy Press, 2010), 36.

during a High Mass. The priest uses a thurible, a brass instrument, often gold-plated, hanging from a chain to disperse burning incense about the altar. The practice goes back to the rituals of the temple. "The priest shall also put some of the blood on the horns of the altar of fragrant incense which stands before the LORD in the tent of meeting" (Leviticus 4:7). The altar represents Christ and contains the relics of saints. The incense shows reverence, symbolizes the sanctifying grace of the Holy Spirit, and the prayers of the saints, as well. "Let my prayer be incense before you; my uplifted hands an evening offering" (Psalm 141:2). We also incense on the altar on earth in imitation of the angels in heaven: "Another angel came and stood at the altar, holding a gold censer. He was given a great quantity of incense to offer, along with the prayers of all the holy ones, on the gold altar that was before the throne" (Apoc. 8:3).

4. Introit

In the picture on the foyer back wall (4) we saw an old car with a sign that said "Made in Detroit," though the "Made in," and the "D" in Detroit, had all but faded away. This was to recall the sounds of the word "Introit." The Latin word means "entrance," and the priest, having ascended the altar, reads the proper (changing) prayer of the Introit from the "epistle side" (the left side of the altar from the perspective of the altar cross, the right side from the congregation's perspective). The missal booklet that I use and referenced earlier refers at this point to Tobias[13] 12:6. That verse reads: "Bless God and give him thanks before all the living for the good things he has done for you, by blessing and extolling his name in song. Proclaim before all with due honor the deeds of God, and do not be slack in thanking him." The particular sample Introit in my missal for the Mass of the Holy Trinity begins, *"Benedicta sit sancta Trinitas,"* "Blessed be the holy Trinity," and includes within it the words of the "Glory Be" prayer, as we heard before during the first part of the Mass in the *Judica Me.*

5. Kyrie

And next you heard those stirring strains of Wagner when at the gun rack in the foyer (location 5) you saw the flight of the *Valkyries.*

---

13 Tobit in the NAB, RSV, and many other translations.

Now we examine the phrase or the song you really do hear at Mass, because it is time for the *Kyrie*. (Indeed, we might as well imagine those *Valkyries* praying the *Kyrie* too!) Here is how the *Kyrie* is prayed in the Latin Mass (recited in Greek):

> Priest: *Kyrie, eleison.*
> Server: *Kyrie, eleison.*
> Priest: *Kyrie, eleison.*
> Server: *Christe eleison.*
> Priest: *Christe eleison.*
> Server: *Christe eleison.*
> Priest: *Kyrie eleison.*
> Server: *Kyrie eleison.*
> Priest: *Kyrie eleison.*

In this prayer, the Church implores for mercy from the Holy Trinity. The first three proclamations of "Kyrie eleison," address the Lord as God the Father, the next three proclamations of "Christe eleison," address the Lord as Christ, God the Son, and the final three proclamations of "Kyrie eleison," address the Lord as the Holy Spirit. As we hear this nine-fold dialogue of prayer between the priest and the server we would do well to recall how it mimics on earth the nine choirs of angels who sing to the Holy Trinity in heaven.

This prayer is called the Kyrie from its original ancient Greek, for Kyrie means, "the Lord." The original Greek for "have mercy," is "eleison.[14] The medieval Dominican theologian and teacher of St. Thomas Aquinas, St. Albert the Great, explained why the Kyrie was traditionally sung in Greek, rather than in Latin. He elaborates on four reasons which are presented here in summary:

1) "First because it was in Greece that the most sublime wisdom flourished, as it is said in the Epistle to the Corinthians: 'The Jews requires signs, and the Greeks seek after wisdom.'"

2) Second it was because of their observance of laws and natural justice, "for as the Jew recognized this justice of the Gospel through faith in the justice of the Mosaic law, so also the Greek discovered the justice of the Gospel through faith in natural justice."

3) The third reason relates to language. The majority of the New Testament had been written in Greek, and the first seven churches were founded in the parts of Asia Minor called Greece.

4) The fourth reason is that the faith came to the Latins from

_____

14 *Christos* is the Greek for *Anointed One* or *Messiah*. They words are pronounced as "kee-**ree**-eh ay-**lay**-ee-sohn; **Krees-**tayay-**lay**-ee-sohn. (The Kyrie is most reverent and beautiful sung in Gregorian chant. I also cannot help but share with you what I'm hearing as I type these words. I recommend that some time, through CD or through the Internet, you listen to the *Kyrie* of Catholic composer Anton Bruckner's Mass No. 1 in D Minor. I find the *Kyrie,* the *Agnus Dei*, and all of the prayers of this Mass rendered most hauntingly and reverently. For a more rousing version, try the *Kyrie* of Mozart's famous Requiem Mass. Indeed, many of the greatest classical composers including Beethoven, Tchaichovksy, and others, have written beautiful Masses that can be listened to with spiritual profit while you read about, memorize, and contemplate the Mass!)

Greece, whence Sts. Peter and Paul had travelled first. The words of the *Kyrie Eleison*, "Lord, have mercy," recall that the Greeks were the first of the Gentiles to receive from Paul and Barnabas the grace of Salvation (Acts 13). "That this same grace was borne from Greece into the West, we preserve in the words and syllables which that people first used to implore the mercy of God."[15]

Let us always implore devoutly of Christ the Lord that he will indeed shower us with his divine mercy, especially as we prepare to receive Him in holy Mass.

6. Gloria

Next, we moved to the center of the foyer (6) where we saw the famous singer, dear friend, or even the old flag that reminded us of the Gloria "*Gloria in excelsis Deo*," the priest begins, "et in terra pax homnibus bonae voluntatis." "Glory be to God on high and on earth peace to men of good will."

As we move from the Penitential Rite to the Gloria, our focus moves from our own sinfulness and unworthiness to the majesty of God who so graciously cleanses our sins and so generously showers graces upon us. We echo the angels rejoicing at Christ's birth with the first line of this prayer: "Glory to God in the highest and peace on earth to those on whom his favor rests" (Luke 2:14). Indeed, it

---

15 As summarized in Kevin Vost, *St. Albert the Great: Champion of Faith and Reason* (Charlotte, NC: TAN Books, 2011), 140-141.

first appeared at the nighttime Christmas Mass around 128 A.D., when Pope St. Telesphorus proclaimed: "at the opening of the sacrifice the angelic hymn should be repeated – that is, 'Glory to God in the highest!'"[16] Further, the priest extends, raises, and then joins his hands at the start of the glorious prayer as a gesture invoking the angels themselves to assist in this great prayer of praise to God.

Since the Gloria is a joyous song of praise, it is omitted during the seasons of Advent and Lent because in Advent we await Christ's coming, and in Lent we meditate upon Christ's sufferings as we await his Passion and Resurrection. During most Sundays of the year, though, we recite this glorious prayer in praise and gratitude to God, reciting a litany of his titles and attributes as declared in the Scriptures – as Lord and King, and also as Father, Son, and Holy Spirit, paying tribute to the mystery of the Holy Trinity. The middle lines briefly recapitulate the story of Jesus Christ, the eternally begotten Son who came into the world to offer himself as the Lamb of God to expiate our sins, and who sits eternally at the right hand of God the Father. The next time we hear this prayer, let us linger on the meaning of every single word, thanking and praising God with every syllable of our speech and with every fiber of our being.

Please see a missal, or better yet, attend Latin Mass to hear this glorious prayer of praise and thanks to God.

---

16 Cited in Cardinal Donald Wuerl & Mike Aquilina, *The Mass: The Glory, The Mystery, The Tradition* (New York: Image, 2013), 106-107.

7. Collect

Up in the foyer's chandelier (7) we found a collection basket brimming over not with money, but with prayers. For the third location in a row, the old Latin Mass parallels the new vernacular Mass, for here we come again to the Collect or the Opening Prayer, that four-parted prayer that calls upon God the Father or the Son, recalls one of God's great deeds, makes a request of God, and declares that our prayer is made through Christ's mediation. This prayer is a proper that changes with each Mass. The missal that I use provides an example that begins with the words "Omnipotens semperne Deus," "Almighty and Everlasting God." Let's read it right now in English, watching for those four parts, and praising the almighty God all the while:

> Almighty and Everlasting God, by Whose gift Thy servants, in cofessing the true Faith, acknowledge the glory of the Eternal Trinity, and adore the Unity in the power of Thy Majesty: grant that by steadfastness in the same Faith we may evermore be defended from all adversities. Through our Lord Jesus Christ Thy Son, Who liveth and reigneth with Thee in the unity of the Holy Ghost, God for everand ever. Server: Amen.

8. Epistle

Here, at the site of the foyer's mirror (8) we saw a letter with pistol with a large "E" on it,and that "*E pistol*" is there merely to remind us of the Epistle. In the Traditional Latin Mass, at least for the last one thousand years or so, there has only been one Scripture reading prior to the Gospel, and that from the New Testament, most often from the letters (i.e., epistles) of St. Paul. It is read, as you might suspect, from the epistle side of the altar while the congregation sits. It is also a proper reading that changes with each Mass according to the day of the liturgical season.

So then, so far, the words of the Prophet David have prepared the ascent to the altar and an apostle has spoken to us of the Word of God. Very soon within the order of the Mass we'll hear the words of the Word Himself.

9. Gradual

Underneath the mirror upon the cushioned bench (9), you will recall your friend Al wearing a graduation cap and gown and climbing up some steps. Now let's see what he was doing there. The graduate Al was climbing those steps to remind us of the *Gradual*. The Gradual is another proper prayer that changes with each Mass, but in each variation it prepares us for the Gospel and gained its named from the Gradual Psalms which the ancient Jews would sing as they climbed up the steps of the Temple. The example provided in the missal booklet I use (from the Solemnity of the Most Holy Trinity) starts, "*Benedictus es, Domine, qui intueris abyssos, et sedes super Cherubim,*" "Blessed art Thou, O Lord, that beholdest the depths and sittest above the Cherubim." (Daniel 3:55 in the Vulgate).

What beautiful, heavenly imagery here! It calls to mind quite clearly again that the Mass recapitulates the heavenly Mass of the angels and saints, where God sits above the nine choirs of angels, the Cherubim being those of the second highest rank.[17]

10. Alleluia (or Tract)

In the small drawer of the cushioned bench we saw Al again and this time with Lulu. They are there of course, to remind us of the Alleluia. It goes *"Alleluia, alleluia. Benedictus es Domine, Deus partum nostrorum, et laudabilis in saecula. Alleluia,"* which is rendered in English "Alleluia, alleluia. Blessed art Thou, O Lord, the God of our fathers, and worthy to be praised for ever. Alleluia." Keeping the heavenly nature of the Holy Mass in mind, we might do well to recall the multitudes in heaven, proclaiming again and again around God's throne a full four times, *"Alleluia! Alleluia! Alleluia! Alleluia!"* (Revelation 19:1, 3, 4, & 6).

You might recall as well the Al and Lulu were on a train track. The track reminds us of the Tract, a prayer that is used in lieu of the *Allelulia* during mournful seasons such as Lent. Its name comes from the Latin word *tractus* meaning flowing or continuous, and it is often excerpted from one of the Psalms.

---

17 The highest tier consists of the Seraphim, Cherubim, and Thrones, the middle tier consisting of the Dominions, Thrones, and Virtues, and the last of the Principalities, Archangels, and Angels. For as fascinating look at these choirs of angels, building upon the writings of the Scriptures, Dionysius, and Pope St. Gregory the Great, see St. Thomas Aquinas' *Summa Theologica,* I, Q. 108.

11. Sequence

Recall now the shower of golden sequins raining down in the center of the living room (11). Medieval monks composed many beautiful pious poems that continued after the tract. These prayers come to be known as the Sequence, since they follow on from the Tract, but only during certain liturgical feasts of the year: Five retained in the 1962 missal to be recited or sung in the Mass are the *Victimae Paschali* at Easter, the *Veni Sancte Spiritus* at Pentecost, the *Lauda Sion* for Corpus Christi; the *Stabat Mater* for Our Lady of Sorrows and the *Dies Irae* for Requiem Masses.The *Dies Irae* (Day of Wrath) is about Christ's Second Coming and Judgment). Fr. Jackson reports that the "*Dies Irae* is considered by many to be the most magnificent hymn ever composed for the Church. It is a perfect work of art.[18]

12. Gospel

And now we come to the words of the Word, the Gospel of our Lord Jesus Christ. This is why we saw our good news boy through the picture window (12) proclaiming good news out in the back yard. Moving from our memory tour back to the church and the Holy Mass, the priest's missal has now been moved the right, Gospel side of the altar (the left from our perspective in the nave). The priest,

---

18 *Nothing Superfluous*, p. 156. (The *Dies Irae* is magnificent in Gregorian chant. For a very famous and moving rendition of the *Dies Irae* by a classical composer, listen sometime to the rousing *Dies Irae* of Mozart's *Requiem Mass* in D Minor.)

bowed and with hands joined in prayer, first recites a prayer known as the "*Munda Cor Meum.*" Picture him, if you'd like, rubbing a bar of soap over his heart, because these words mean "cleanse my heart." The pure of heart will see God (Matt. 5:8), and the pure of heart will proclaim his Gospel as well. His call for cleansing and purification also include the cleansing of his lips, recalling the words of Isaiah 6:5-7. Here, in English, are the words of the prayer:

> Cleanse my heart and my lips, O Almighty God, Who didst cleanse the lips of the prophet Isasis with a burning coal; through Thy gracious mercy so purify me that I may worthily proclaim the holy Gospel, through Christ Our Lord. Amen.

> Grant, O Lord, Thy blessing.

> May the Lord be in my heart and on my lips that I may worthily and fittingly proclaim His Gospel. Amen.

Next, the priest prepares to read the day's Gospel (typically in English in American Latin Masses), saying "*Dominus vobiscum,*" "The Lord be with you," to which the server answers "*Et cum spiritu tuo*" "And with your spirit." The priest recites from which book today's Gospel comes, and as in the *Novus Ordo*, crosses his forehead, lips, and heart, and we do likewise with him, honoring the Gospel and praying that our intellect, speech, and hearts be blessed by it.

After reading the Gospel, the priest delivers a homily or sermon, meditating upon the day's readings and perhaps the saint whose feast is on that day. Preaching is such an important act to call people to Christ, to catechize the faithful, and to stir listeners to live out the

Gospel message. In the early 1200s, there was a crisis of preaching of sorts in the Church that was addressed at the Lateran Council of 1215. Typically only bishops were preaching regular homilies, and homilies were therefore rare. Rising to the occasion were two new holy religious Orders, St. Francis' Friars Minor, and St. Dominic's order, so focused on preaching that it would be declared the Order of Preachers.

Drawing a bit (two bits actually) from medieval Dominican wisdom on preaching, I'll note that Blessed Humbert of Romans, the order's fifth Master General, wrote an extensive treatise *On the Formation of Preachers* that examines the art and grace of preaching from every imaginable angle. Here is one small bit of his sage advice:

> Preachers will keep their sermons of reasonable length as well, so they don't give their hearers indigestion! Some preach with nothing but *rational arguments*, others with nothing but *anecdotes*, and yet others by citing *authorities*. The good preacher does all three in the right proportions. Indeed, when all three work together, the "hook of preaching" hangs from a strong triple line, "a line which no fish can easily break."[19]

Blessed Humbert's contemporary, the patron saint of science, the teacher and mentor of Saint Thomas Aquinas, the Bishop of Regensburg, and one of the Doctors of the Church,[20] Saint Albert the Great,

---

19 Kevin Vost, *Hounds of the Lord: Great Dominican Saints Every Catholic Should Know and Love* (Manchester, NH: Sophia Institute Press, 2015), 42, with quotations citing Simon Tugwell's *Early Dominicans* (New York: Paulist Press, 1980).

20 (How's that for an introduction?)

reportedly preached homilies that were brief and consisted of three main parts:

(1) a short and straightforward literal explanation of a scriptural passage,

(2) an *allegorical* and *mystical interpretation* of the passage, and

(3) a summary of the message in clear-cut language, often cast in the form of an easily memorized prayer that God would grant the congregation the spiritual fruits that should accrue from pondering and applying his sacred lessons.[21]

Even if the homily we hear at Mass should not be expounded from the likes of a Blessed Humbert or a Saint Albert the Great, we would do well to recall that the priest before us appears in *persona Christi,* in the person of Christ, with words guided by the Holy Spirit. We need to listen carefully then to discern God's message for each of us at each Mass.

13. Credo

At our last location within this chapter, we saw those professional fates sitting upon the living room sofa (13), presenting what we thought was a very nice scene. Those fates represent the Profession of Faith, the nice scene, the Nicene Creed, which begins with the words, "I believe," which in Latin is simply *"Credo."* The priest

---

21 For those who might care to learn more about St. Albert's great homiletics and more, see the chapter on St. Albert in my *Hounds of the Lord,* or St. Albert's complete biography in my *St. Albert the Great: Champion of Faith and Reason* (Charlotte, NC: TAN Books, 2011).

recites the Credo during Sunday Mass and principal feasts. As he come to the words "and by the Holy Spirit was incarnate of the Virgin Mary, and became man," the priest and congregation genuflect when he recites the words, "*Et incarnates est de Spirito Sancto ex Maria Virgine et Homo Factus est.*" At the prayer's end, the priest declares, "*Dominus vobiscum*" "The Lord be with you," the server responds "*Et cum spiritu tuo,*" "And with thy spirit" and then the priest says "*Oremus*" (Let us pray.)

And now this chapter has all but ended, so too has the "Mass of the Catechumens." In ancient times those who had not yet joined the Catholic Church would be dismissed at this point in the Mass, right before the Commencement of the "Mass of the Faithful." In our next chapter we turn to that most holy and faith-filled part of the Latin Mass, but first let's remember something very important about memory itself.

Repetitio Est Mater Memoriae[22]

Before we move on to the Mass of the Faithful in this book, please note that a hallmark of true memorization is the passage of material from the fleeting capacities of short-term memory into the almost limitless stores of our long-term memories. Long-term storage is demonstrated when one can recall material after a significant delay. It has probably been several minutes now since we entered the memory house and encountered the first thirteen locations and im-

---

22 Repetition is the mother of memory.

ages housed within the foyer and living room. Recall then, if you will, those first thirteen locations, their images, and the parts of the Mass that they represent. Do you have them all? If yes, good show! (And can you name them backwards, from 13 back to 1?) If not, then rehearse them again using the summary table in this chapter and give them another go. When you've got them all down, rehearse them again the next time before you actually go to Mass. Linger on the words of each prayer as well, and with focused attention and weekly or daily repetition, eventually they, too, will be written on the tablet of your heart.

— PART 2 —

MASS OF THE FAITHFUL

*For from the rising of the sun to its setting my name is great among the nations,
and in every place incense is offered to my name, and a pure offering; from my
name is great among the nations, says the LORD of hosts.*

Malachi 1:11

Still within the living room and right in front of the sofa, we find,
as one might expect, a coffee table (location 14), but you probably did
not expect to see a 17th Century British *Tory* sitting on it waiting for
you to *offer* him not tea and crumpets, but some *bread and wine.* Next
we come to the location of the big-screen television set (15) and you
are surprised to see a vast cloud of sweet *incense* rise up from it. On
now to the fireplace (16) and instead of a set of logs you find a large
bowl of steaming volcanic *lava* and you are astonished to see that it's
labeled *"for washing hands."* (Undoubtedly, not many germs would sur-

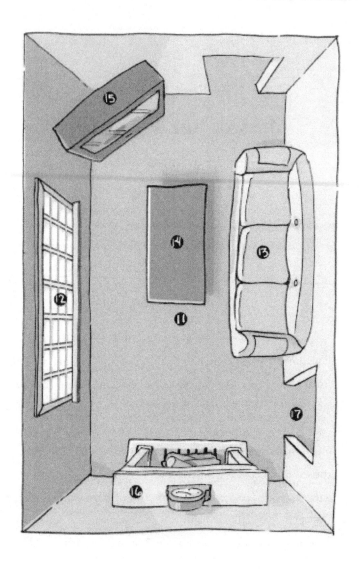

vive!) At the living room doorway into the dining room (17), as you might have suspected, you see your friend, *Sue,* her little dog *Skippy,* and *Santa Claus* himself eating a *Trinidad* candy.[1]

And now we enter the dining room of the Mass of the Faithful. At the dining room doorway (18), you find a boat *oar,* a hot cup of *latte,* and a couple *fraternity brothers.* Got all that?

At the foot of the dining room table (19) you recognize your own parish *priest's face.* On the center of the table (20), as opposed to up on the housetop, you see a walrus drinking some freeze-dried coffee (*Sanka* to be precise) and he's got some on his *tusk.* And that takes care of this chapter's memory tour. Let's see now how we've done with our memory work, and let's take a peek at just what we have really remembered.

14. Coffee table	*You offer Tory bread and wine*	Offertory
15. Television	*Cloud of incense rises*	Incensing altar, etc.
16. Fireplace	*Lava bowl for washing hands*	Lavabo
17. Living room doorway	*Sue, Skippy, & Santa eat a Trindad*	Suscipe, Sancta Trinitas
18. Dining room doorway	*Oar, latte, frat brothers*	Orate Fratres

---

1 So maybe you didn't expect that. Not familiar with the Trinidad? Invented by the Fanny May Confections in 1970, it features a dark, creamy chocolate center covered by a golden toasted coconut shell. Try one some time, but not while fasting before Mass!

19. Foot of table	*Your priest's face*	Preface
20. Center of table	*Sanka, tusk*	Sanctus

14. Offertory

Still within the living room and right in front of the sofa, we found, as one might expect, a coffee table (location 14), though the rite represented predates coffee drinking by a good thousand years or more! Here we saw a British Tory whom we offered not tea, but bread and wine. This unusual scene should serve well to call to mind the right of the *Offertory,* wherein the priest asks God to receive his offering of bread and wine as Christ Himself offered them. The Offertory begins the Mass of the Faithful and the priest beings from the middle of the altar with a proper (changing) Offertory Verse. A sample in the missal booklet I use starts *"Benedictus sit Deus Pater…"* "Blessed be God, the Father…" After this brief *Offertory Verse,* the servers ring a set of bells once, and the priest commences with a series of gestures and prayers that I'll summarize below, for the sake of space, giving only the first few words in Latin, their English translation, and a suggestion for memorization:[2]

---

2 I would suggest that you move toward this level of memorization, if you are so inclined, only *after* you have mastered the basic 42 parts of this Mass. Of course you would do this with the help of a missal, reading the complete prayers and meditating upon their meanings.

Gestures & First Latin Words	English Translation	Suggested Keyword Images for Sound and Meaning
The priest raises the paten with host saying:		
Suscipe, Sancte Pater…	Accept, O Holy Father…	*Sue, Skippy,* and a *saintly potter* ask their father to accept a gift.
Priest makes Sign of Cross (+) with paten and places host on corporal. Moves to right side of altar, pouring wine and water into chalice, blessing it before mixed, saying:		
Deus + qui humanae substantiae…	O God, + Who in creating man…	*Deuce* card and *key* are handed to a *human* God just gave *substance* to
Returning to the altar's middle, the priest now offers the chalice to God, saying		
Offerimus Tibi…	We offer unto Thee…	You *offer God* an *emus' tibia* bone and a holy chalice

Priest makes + with chalice, places it on corporal, covers it with pall and bowing, says:		
In Spiritu Humilitas...	Humbled in Spirit...	You feel *in* you the stirrings of the Holy *Spirit* while *you* eat some *hummus*
The priest raises his eyes and hands and says:		
Veni, Sanctificator omnipotens...	Come Thou, the Sanctifier...	You see a *veiny Saint* from *Decatur* who *on* his *knee* holds *patens* and who looks all powerful.

The actions and prayers of this part of the Mass are as all other parts, reflective of scriptural origins, and rich in many levels of meaning. In the prayer beginning *Suscipe Sancte*, for example, consider that the words *"pro omnibus fidelibus christianis vivis atque defunctis,"* "for all faithful Christians, living and dead," proclaim that not only does the Mass honor God, it offers blessings not only to all Christians living, but also to the dead, reminiscent of the first scriptural reference to prayers for the dead in 2 Maccabees 12:42-45. The mixing of the water and wine, for another example, represents the human and divine natures of Christ. The water suggests the water that flowed from the side of Christ as the wine represents the blood. As for some additional scriptural roots, note well that in the prayer that commences with *In Spiritu Humilitas,* the words that ask God to find favor with our sacrifice this day reference Daniel 3:39-40: "But with contrite heart and humble spirit let us be received; as though it were burnt offerings of rams and bulls, or tens of thousands of fat lambs, so let our sacrifice be in your presence today and find favor before you; for those who trust in you cannot be put to shame."

We would do well to reflect here, too, about what goes on with us in the pews while the great offertory goes on at the altar. When that collection basket is passed, we are provided as well with the opportunity to express and to grow in more than one heavenly virtue.

Gratitude is an obvious one. God has given us everything that we are, and all that we have, and indeed sustains us in existence every moment of our being. Will our monetary offering the next time at Mass express a true heartfelt gratitude?

Another less obvious virtue is that of *magnificence.* The word derives from the Latin *magnus* for "great" and *facere* for "to do or make." Will the contribution we offer up to God at Mass help do and make great things for the glory of God and the aid of our neighbor? It need not be huge, but proportionate to how we abundantly have been gifted with wealth, as we saw in the case of the heavenly weight of the poor widow's penny (Mark 12:41-44; Luke 21:1-4).

15. Incensing altar, etc.

Back now to our memory house's living room and you'll recall that at the site of the big screen TV (15) we saw a great cloud of incense arise. This image reminds us of the priest's blessing of the incense and the incensing of the offerings of the bread and wine, of the crucifix and the altar, while reciting prayers, including Psalm 140 [141], which talks about prayers being like incense before God.

The incensing takes place only at High Mass. Dom Gueringer's book on the *Explanation of the Holy Mass* highlights the fact that many things go along this rite with the section heading entitled "Incensing the Altar, etc." If you'd like to recall the "etc.," I can hardly hear the word without thinking of the musical *The King and I*. The Siamese King learns and develops a love for the Latin word *"etcetera,"* and ends almost all of his declamations, *"Etcetera, etcetera, etcetera!"* (If the King of Siam can help us remember one way we honor the King of Kings, well, I'm all for calling him to mind.)

16. Lavabo

On now to the fire place (16) with that fiery bowl of molten lava marked "for washing your hands." Now this image may not sound so extreme for those familiar with that heavy duty hand-cleanser Lava Soap, made with actual pumice (lava rock). What is important, of course, is not our image, but what it represents. *"Lavabo"* means "I will wash." It is the first word of the prayer the priest recites as he washes his hands to symbolize the purity and cleanliness needed to take part in such a holy sacrifice.

"*Lavabo inter innocentes manus meas: et circumdabo altare tuum, Domine...*", "I will wash my hands among the innocent, and I will encompass Thine Altar, O Lord..." The words of this prayer echo Psalm 25 [26]:6-12, and end with the Glory Be.

We would do well to meditate upon the symbolism of cleansing and purity of the hands. Let's consider for a minute this story from the ancient Irish lore surrounding St. Brigid of Kildare (453-525 AD):

> Out in the fields of Curragh, on one fine summer day, a young student named Ninnidh went running past Brigid at breakneck speed. When asked where he was going, he told her, "I'm going to heaven!" Brigid recited the "Our Father" with him and prophesied that he would become a priest one day and would administer to her the holy viaticum of the Eucharist upon her own deathbed. The formerly frivolous youth devoted himself

to his studies and grew steadily toward saintliness. From that day on he would wear a glove on the hand that would deliver to Ireland's patroness her last Communion. This is why he was called Lamh-Gland, "Ninnidh of the clean hand."[3]

We might ask ourselves if we are doing all that we can to keep our hands and our hearts clean for when we receive Jesus for the next time, let alone for our last time on earth?

17. Suscipe, Sancta, Trinitas

Moving along to the living room doorway (17) you saw that odd scene of Sue, Skippy, and Santa Claus eating a Trinidad chocolate. They are there to remind us of the Latin words *"Suscipe, Sancta, Trinitas."* We might imagine them also handing something, perhaps one of those Trinidads, to the Holy Trinity, because those words mean, "Receive, Holy Trinity." These are the first words of the next prayer in the Mass, the Prayer to the Most Holy Trinity. It spells out the reasons for the holy offering in beautiful words well worth presenting here in full translation:

> Receive, O Holy Trinity, this oblation which we make to Thee in memory of the Passion, Resurrection and Ascension of our Lord Jesus Christ; and in honor of blessed Mary ever Virgin, of blessed John the Baptist, the holy Apostles Peter and Paul, of these and of all the Saints. To them let it bring honor, and to us

---

3 Kevin Vost, *Three Irish Saints: A Guide to Finding Your Spiritual Style* (Charlotte, NC: TAN Books, 2011), 151.

salvation, and may they whom we are commemorating here on earth deign to plead for us in heaven. Through the same Christ our Lord. Amen.

18. Orates Fratres

Over the threshold and into the dining room doorway (18) and now we'll recall the oar and the frat brothers sipping on latte because this will call to mind the *Orates Fratres.* Picture them praying, too, because these words mean "Pray, brethren." This prayer that our sacrifice "may be acceptable to God the Father Almighty." The server voices (in Latin) the words:

> May the Lord accept the Sacrifice from thy hands, to the praise and glory of His Name, for our benefit and for that of all His holy Church. Priest (in a low voice): *Amen.*

The priest then quietly recites the Secrets (a proper, changing prayer that asks that God make our offering may be perfect), and it ends with a dialogue between the priest and server:

Priest (aloud): *Per omnia saecula saecolorum.* (World without end.)

The people now stand.

Server: *Amen.*

Priest: *Dominus vobiscum.* (The Lord be with you.)

Server: *Et cum spiritu tuo.* (And with your spirit.)

Priest: *Sursum corda.* (Lift up your hearts.)

Server: *Habeamus ad Dominum.* (We have lifted them up to the Lord.)

Priest: *Gratias agamus Domino Deo nostro.* (Let us give thanks to the Lord, Our God.)

Server: *Dignum et justum est.* (It is right and just.)

19. Preface

At the chair at the foot of the dining room table (19), you saw your own priest's face to remind you of the Preface. This prayer changes during different liturgical seasons. The one in the missal booklet I use begins *"Vere dignum et justum…"* "It is truly meet and just…" It serves to proclaim thanksgiving and praise to the Father, the Son, and the Holy Spirit.

20. Sanctus

Next, at the center of the dining room table (20), was that freeze-dried coffee Sanka on a walrus' tusk. The sounds of the words Sanka and tusk will remind us of the *Sanctus*, and if you'd like to lock in the meaning as well, imagine that Sanka's written label thrice pays homage to God, calling him *"Sanctus, Sanctus, Sanctus,"* "Holy, Holy, Holy…" Here is what the priest acclaims (translated) in the Latin Mass. After the bells ring three times, the priest bows with hands joined, while all of the congregation kneels:

Holy, Holy, Holy, Lord God of Hosts. Heaven and earth are full of Thy Glory. Hosanna in the highest. + Blessed is He Who cometh in the name of the Lord. Hosanna in the highest.

It is so fitting to proclaim "Hosanna," praise in the highest be to the Lord in heaven, who is about to come join us on earth through the rites He gave us that immediately follow.

Before we proceed, though, it's time to slow down a bit and see how we are progressing in writing anew the Old Mass on the tablets of our hearts. Please check the summary tables in this and the previous chapter, along with the illustrations, or the master table in Appendix A. Do you have them all now, all of the first 20 parts? If you do, congratulations! You are almost half-way there! If not, why not rehearse until you have them locked in, ready to unlock the next time you attend Latin Mass?

— Part 3 —

Canon of the Mass

Silence now reigns at the altar. In the Old Law the high priest alone entered into the Holy of holies. Like Moses, he spoke alone with God, and the Lord answered him. (Cf. Ex. 19, 10.) Thus, too, the priest recites in silence the wonderful prayers of the Canon, and renews the mysterious sacrifice of Christ's infinite love.

Rev. F. X. Lasance, The New Roman Missal[1]

On now to that wall thermometer (location 21) and peering inside you see (and hear) a most unusual scene. A British gentleman has just fired loudly a little toy *canon*. He's apparently signaling his staff that it's tea time, because a servant immediately responds with great gusto, *"Tea, I get 'er!"* Back now to the seat on the right at the dining

---

1 Fr. F. X. Lasance, *The New Roman Missal: In Latin and English* (Palmdale, CA: Christian Book Club of America, 1993), 86.

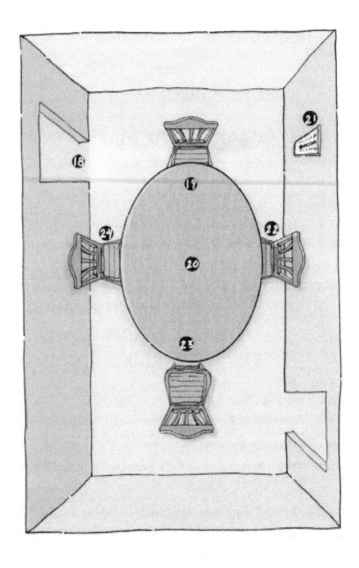

room table (22), and here we see what appears to be a statue of the memory goddess *Mnemosyne*,[2] but when you see her *toe* move, you figure she's really *alive!* On we go now to the head of the table (23) as we complete this chapter's briefest of memory tours. There you see Lenin, Stalin, Mao-Tse Tung, and Fidel Castro all trying to sit down in the chair as if in a game of musical chairs and the music has just stopped, and all the while they seem to be counting some objects on the table in front of them. So, to put it in a nutshell, our image here, believe it or not, needs to be *Communists counting*. Now let's get down to business and see what all of this means.

21. Thermometer	*Canon blasts/ "Tea, I get' er."*	Te Igitur
22. Seat on right	*Mnemosyne's toe moves*	Memento of the Living
23. Head of table	*Communists counting*	Communicantes

21. Te Igitur

How come when we peered inside the wall thermometer (21) we heard a canon blast and a British butter, declare, "Tea, I'll get 'er!"?

---

2 *Mnemosyne,* or Memory, was said to be the "Mother of the Muses," the mother of nine goddesses representing epic poetry, history, music, lyric poetry, tragedy, hymns, dance, comedy, and astronomy, since all depend upon memory for their perfection. Her name is carried on in our words *mnemonic* and *mnemonics* as an adjective referring to memory aiding effects or a noun referring to the memory aids themselves. In this book, we use mnemonic techniques which themselves can be called mnemonics.

Well, of course to remind us of the Canon of the Mass and the prayer that begins, *"Te Igitur."* *Canon* is a Latin word meaning "a measure, standard, or rule," and in the context of the Mass, it begins with the prayer beginning *"Te Igitur"* (To You)[3] and concludes at the Communion Rite with the *Pater Noster* (Our Father). The holy prayers and actions of the Canon include the prayers of Consecration, but to avoid an overly long chapter, for the lessons of memory are digested best in small servings, this chapter will include the Prayers before Consecration, and the next chapter the Prayers of Consecration themselves.

The *Te Igitur* begins *"Te Igitur, clementissime Pater, per Jesum Christum Filium tuum, Dominum nostrum, supplices rogamus ac petimus...,* ("To You, most merciful Father, we humbly pray and beseech Thee, through Je-

---

3 If you'd like to remember that *Te Igitur* begins this prayer with the first translated words of "To You," simply imagine that when the butler presents the tea, he simply says, "To you."

sus Christ Thy Son, Our Lord…") Though our mnemonic device included the sound of a canon blast, note well that this prayer is actually uttered inaudibly by the priest while he bows before the altar. He asks God that our sacrifice to Him, through Christ, be acceptable and bring benefits of peace and unity to all within the Church, together with the pope and local bishop, and all who believe in the Catholic faith.

The *Te Igitur* is so rich in meaning that throughout many centuries, it was considered most significant that the very letter "T" with which it begins, the *"Tau"* of ancient Hebrew, is the form of Christ's cross. Even in the Old Testament, Ezekiel (9:4-6) had written that God would save those with the mark of the *tau* on their foreheads. Observe your own copy of the Missal for the Latin Mass, and you are very likely to see above the *Te Igitur* a pictorial depiction of Christ on the cross. In the days of "illuminated," or decorated books, the letter "T" itself of *Te Igitur* was often drawn as Christ upon the cross.

22. Memento of the Living

Next at the chair on the right (22), we observed the Greek goddess Mnemosyne, wiggling her toe, so we concluded she was living. Mnemosyne and the wiggling toe are simply there to help us remember the *Memento of the Living*. Next in the prayer before consecration the priest continues silently, *"Memento Domine, famulorum famularumque tuarum"* (Be mindful, O Lord, of Thy servants and handmaids…"). Here, the priest prays for the pope and bishop and all gathered at the Mass, declaring that the sacrifice is offered in praise of God and for the redemption of the souls, the health, and well-being of the faithful still living on earth.

23. Communicantes

Next, at the head of the table (23) we saw that unlikely scene of some infamous Communists counting something before them. Those Communists counting are simply there to remind us of the prayer that begins *"Communicantes."* Of course, no Communists are invoked in this prayer, but the holy communion of all the saints. Here, the priest silently begins, *"Communicantes, et memoriam venerantes, in primus gloriosae semper Virginis Mariae, Genetricis Dei et Domini nostri Jesu Christi...."* ("In Communion with, and honoring the memory in the first place of the glorious ever Virgin Mary Mother of our God and Lord Jesus Christ...") St. Joseph is next invoked, along with various Apostles and Martyrs who are specifically named, both from apostolic times and from the early centuries of the Church.[4]

Clearly, as we prepare for the mystery of the consecration, the Church Militant, those of us still on earth, by no means act alone,

---

4 They are Peter and Paul (named together as joint founders of the Church), Andrew, James, John, Thomas, James, Philip, Bartholomew, Matthew, Simon and Thaddeus (Apostles), Linus, Cletus, Clement (all bishops of Rome ordained by Peter), Sixtus (Sixtus II, another early pope, whose deacon was St. Lawrence,) Cornelius (an early martyred pope), Cyprian (martyred Bishop of Carthage in North Africa), Lawrence (martyred deacon), Chrysogonus (martyred under Emperor Diocletian), John and Paul (martyred under Emperor Julian the Apostate), and Cosmas and Damian (twin physicians martyred under Diocletian whose remains are in Rome.)

but in the company of the Church Triumphant, of the host of God's saints with Him in heaven. The priest asks God that through their merits and prayers we may be guarded and helped by His protection, through Christ our Lord, He concludes with *"Amen."*

Do you now know in order the parts of the Canon of the Prayers Before Consecration? If not, it should take just a minute or two, to peruse the table and picture and lock them all in. We've earned the brief respite this short chapter brings. In the next chapter we'll be taxed with 10 parts of the Mass, those all-crucial prayers through which Christ Himself joins us at Mass in Body and Blood, Soul and Divinity.

— Part 4 —

Consecration Rites

Hoc est enim corpus meum. Hoc est enim calix sanguinis mei.

Jesus Christ[1]

The seat on the left of the dining room table (24) conjures up a very moving scene (literally moving). The chair is transformed into the front seat of a car, and there you are as the passenger while Ichabod Crane is giving you a night time ride right through Sleepy Hollow. You see a good friend that both of you know, so you yell out, *"Honk, Ich. It's her!"* Now that makes a lot of sense, no? Well, we'll see in just a bit. We move now to the door of our family room (25). There just inside stands a *monk* holding up an *O*-shaped *plate* with an *"M"* on it. Something about his demeanor gives you some *qualms* about his in-

---

1 Cf. 1: Cor. 11:24-25, Vulgate

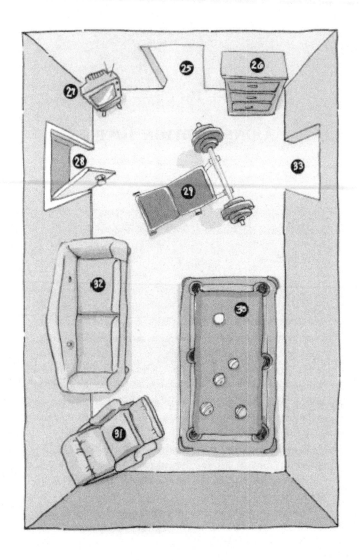

tentions. Sitting upon the dresser (26) you are surprised to see a *priest* in the most ornate vestments you have ever seen. It occurs to you that he looks like Christ and he's *raising a host* with a most striking look of *reverence and awe.* And also, just as he does so, you hear some bells ringing, too. On next to the site of the television set (27), and it bears an image of that same *priest*, now *raising a chalice* over his head with the same *reverence and awe,* and the same bells are ringing, too.

Now you open up the closet (28), and on a stand rests a statue of *Mnemosyne,* but more striking by far *underneath* it is a statue of our *Lord, Jesus Christ.* Next we move to the weight bench (29), and who should be there all in blue, red, and yellow but *Superman* himself, bench-pressing the hugest barbell you've even seen, and he tells you that he'll show you the *proper way!*

Next we move on to the pool table (30), where we see some *supplies* laid out for us -- namely, *tea* and beef *Stroganoff.* Next to the pool table is that comfortable recliner (31), and here yet again is old *Mnemosyne.* This time though her toe does not move and neither does anything else. In fact, it appears she is *dead, and she is in a casket.*

Get ready for this next batch of images because it will take some explaining. Next to the recliner is the family room couch (32), and here we see a group of nobles, yelling out that they have just witnessed a powerful chest muscle (a pectoral) tear wide open a bus (perhaps it was Superman's pectoral!). The image you see then is *nobles quoting "Pec tore a bus!"* Taken back a bit by this room's most unusual scenery, you are relieved to see at the doorway out, a most beautiful *Queen* who says to you, *"Hey, come near!"*

Let's see if we have this group of 10 new images now, from 24 – 33.

24. Seat on left	*"Honk, Ich(abod). It's her!"*	Hanc Igitur
25. Door to family room	*Quams about a monk with O-shaped plate with "M."*	Quam Oblationem
26. Dresser	*Priest in awe raises host, bells*	Consecration of the Host
27. Television	*Priest in awe raises chalice, bells*	Consecration of the Wine
28. Closet	*Under Mnemoysne is statue of the Lord*	Unde et Memores
29. Weight bench	*Superman shows proper way*	Supra Quae Pro-pitio
30. Pool table	*Supplies: tea, stroganoff*	Supplices te Rog-amus
31. Recliner	*Mnemosyne in casket*	Memento of the Dead
32. Couch	*Nobles quote, "Pec tore a bus!"*	Nobis Quoque Peccatoribus
33. Doorway out	*Per Queen, "Hey, come near!"*	Per Quem Haec Omnia

24. Hanc Igitur

Surely you won't forget that in the chair on the left (24) we saying that literally moving scene of Ichabod Crane driving you in a car through Sleepy Hollow. Seeing a friend you called out "Honk, Ich. It's her!" That's simply because the first Prayer of Consecration begins with the Latin words, "Hanc Igitur," which literally means "This, therefore," and which in the Mass is translated, "We therefore." To add meaning to our mnemonic image, you could imagine Ichabod Crane declaring that since you know that person, "*we therefore* honk at her!" To recall that during the Mass the bells are rung once at the commencement of the prayer, you could imagine the car horn sounds just like church bells. But now we must move to the true deeper meaning in the context of the Mass.

This prayer at the start of the Consecration Prayers announces the *oblation* (offering) of our sacrifice to God and pleads that it be accepted and that it wins for us peace in this world, freedom from damnation, and inclusion in God's holy flock. Dom Gueranger notes that the phrase in the middle -- *"diesque nostros in tua pace disponas,"* ("Order our days in Thy peace,") -- was first invoked by Pope St. Gregory the Great in the sixth century while the city of Rome was under military attack by the Lombards, and the words have been retained since, due not only to the great pope's holiness, but also because, as reported by his Deacon John, that at certain dire occasions, the Holy Spirit would descend in the form of a dove above Pope Gregory's head, whispering instructions about what to say into the pope's ear. The *Hanc Igitur* ends with the priest's words *"per Christum Dominium nostrum. Amen"* ("Through Christ our Lord, Amen.")

25. Quam Oblationem

At the door to the family room (25) we had qualms about that monk with an O-shaped plate with an "M" on it simply to remind us of the sounds of the words, *"Quam Oblationem."* Next, the priest begins to again bless the offerings, beginning *"Quam oblationem Tu, Deus, in omnibus, quaesumus, bene + dictum…"* ("Humbly we pray to Thee, O God, be pleased to make this same offering wholly blessed…" You can imagine the monk with the plate bowing humbly before God, asking that God approve our gifts and that they might be acceptable, becoming for us *"Cor + pus, et San + guis fiat dilectissimi Filii tui Domini nostri Jesu Christi"* ("the Body + and Blood + of Thy dearly beloved Son, our Lord Jesus Christ.").

26. Consecration of the Host

Atop the tall family room dresser (26) we saw a priest who looked like Christ, in the most ornate vestments, hold aloft the host with a look of reverence and awe. This image reminds us of the part of the Canon in which the host is actually consecrated. It begins *"Qui pridie quam pateretur, accepit panem in santas ac venerabiles manus suas…"* ("Who, the day before He suffered, took bread into His Holy and venerable hands…") It concludes with the most powerful words of the priest in the person of Christ, *"HOC EST ENIM CORPUS MEUM"* ("FOR THIS IS MY BODY"), echoing words of Christ Himself, at which time, through the power of God, the bread has indeed become sacramentally the body of our Lord Jesus Christ. The priest then genuflects before Christ and adores the Holy Host as the servers ring the bells once. He stands up and elevates the host so that the congregation may venerate it[2] as the bells ring three times. He places the host on the corporal, genuflects in adoration one more time, and the bells ring once again.

What a sign of such deep reverence we see in that after having touched the consecrated host, the priest keeps his thumb and fingers joined until after Communion, accept when he takes up the host.

27. Consecration of the Wine

At the site of what was first the small TV (27) and is now a small stack of scrolls, we saw the same priest holding aloft the chalice of wine, again hearing bells, to represent of course, the consecration of the wine. The priest begins *"Simili modo postquam coenatum est…"* ("In like manner, after he had supped…" and then the priest recounts how Christ repeated the consecration of the wine in the chalice when it became his blood. He continues aloud *"HIC EST ENIM CALIX SANGUINIS MEI…"* ("FOR THIS IS THE CHALICE OF MY BLOOD…") continuing (in translation) "of the new and eternal testament: the mystery of faith: which shall be shed for you and for many unto the remission of sins." Then the priest says quietly (in translation) "As often as ye shall do these things, ye shall do them in remembrance of Me." Next the priest

---

2 We adore the Body of Christ by silently saying, "My Lord and my God!" echoing the words of St. Thomas the Apostle when he recognized the body of the risen Christ (John 20:28).

genuflects and adores the Precious Blood of Christ. The servers ring the bells once. He stands again and elevates the chalice for the adoration of the congregation,[3] as the bells ring three times. He sets down the chalice, covers it, adores it in genuflection once more, and the bells ring once. The Body and Blood, Soul and Divinity, of our Lord Jesus Christ are now right before us and indeed will soon be within our own bodies and souls. Have we taken the time to consider the mystery, majesty, and astounding generosity of this sacrifice in which we are partaking?

28. Unde et Memores

Recall now that at within the family room closet (28) we saw a statue of *Mnemosyne,* the old Greek goddess of memory, but underneath her was a more beautiful statue of our Lord, Jesus Christ. This was simply to remind us of the first words of the next prayer, *"Undes et memores, Domine,"* (And now, O Lord…"). Christ told us to "do this in remembrance of me" (Luke 24:19; 1 Cor. 11:24), and we are doing just that. The priest with hands extended prays in remembrance of Christ's Passion, Resurrection, and Ascension into heaven, recognizing that it is Christ the victim as well as the risen Christ whom we now glorify. Can we take a minute to let that sink in, that the glorified Christ is present before us?

The priest then joins his hands and makes the Sign of the Cross

---

3 We silently pray, "Be mindful, O Lord, of Thy creature, whom Thou hast redeemed by Thy Most Precious Blood."

five times as we continues *"hostiam + puram, hostiam + sanctam, hostiam + immaculatam, Panem + sanctum vitae aeternae, et Calicem + salutis perpetuae"* ("a Victim + which is pure, a Victim + which is holy, a Victim + which is spotless, the holy Bread + of life eternal, and the Chalice + of everlasting Salvation.").

29. Supra Quae Propitio

As we moved to the inclined weight bench (29) we spied the mighty Superman bench pressing the hugest barbell we'd ever seen and offering to show us the proper way. This is simply a reminder of the opening words of the next prayer, *"Supra Quae Propitio."* (To remember the word *quae* instead of way, you could perhaps imagine on Superman's chest, not a big "S" but a "Q!"[4]) Now back to the Mass itself. His hands extended, the priest begins, *"Supra quae propitio ac sereno vultu respicere digneris…"* ("Deign to look upon them with a favorable and gracious countenance…") The priest asks God to accept the sacrifice of the Mass as he did the sacrifices of the servant Abel, the Patriarch Abraham, and the high priest Melchizedek, all of which are described within the book of Genesis.

30. Supplices Te Rogamus

We saw that the pool table (30) was weighted down with supplies

---

4 In recent Superman movies, by the way, we are told that his symbol is not an "S" for Superman, but is his planet's symbol for "hope." How interesting (to me anyway!) that *spem,* the Latin word for hope, does indeed start with an "s!"

including tea and beef Stroganoff. The sounds of the words of this image are there to remind us of the infinitely more valuable supplies of eternal life which now lie upon the table of the altar. *"Supplices te rogamus, omnipotens Deus: jube haec perferri per manus sancti Angeli tui in sublime altare tuum…"* ("Humbly we beseech Thee, almighty God, to command that these, our offerings, be carried by the hands of Thy holy Angel to Thine Altar on high…") We might picture our supplies being carried to God by an angel to remind us of the meaning of these words and to remind us again that we are not alone at Mass, but are joined by even the angels. The priest bowing down, his hands joined and upon the altar, this prayer continues to ask that we may share in every grace and heavenly blessing by partaking in Christ's Body and Blood.

31. Memento of the Dead

Upon the family room recliner (31) we saw *Mnemosyne* one final time, but this time within a casket. This image of Mnemosyne dead is simply to remind us of the beginning of the prayers after consecration, the Commemoration or *Memento of the Dead.* Standing, hands folder in prayer, the priest begins, *"Memento etiam, Domine…"* ("Be mindful, also O Lord…") and recites by name deceased "servants" and "handmaids" who *"dormiunt in somno pacis"* ("sleep the sleep of peace"). Here we pray for the Church Suffering, that the souls in purgatory will attain *"refrigerii, lucis et pacis,"* (refreshment, light and peace.) At this time we might also recall and pray for our own departed family and friends. As usual with so many of the prayers of the Canon, and because he presides in the person of Christ, the priest concludes: *"Per eundem Christum Dominum nostrum. Amen."* ("Through the same Christ our Lord. Amen.")

32. Nobis Quoque Peccatoribus

Upon the family room couch (32) we saw a sight that contends for the strangest of images in this memory house so full of the most unusual sights. We saw, you will recall, a group of nobles quoting "Pec tore a bus!" imagining that powerful chest muscles (perhaps those of Superman) tore open a bus (most likely to free people trapped inside). The image had to be so odd to suggest in English the Latin words with the next prayer starts, the *"Nobis Quoque Peccatoribus!"* Close enough? So now, what do those words mean?

Calling to mind the pectoral muscles,[5] it is with these first three words alone of all the Canon that the priest declares loudly as he strikes his chest, *"Nobis quoque peccatoribus famulis tuis, de multitudine miserationum tuarum sperantibus..."* (To us also Thy sinful servants, who put our trust in the multitude of Thy mercies...) He prays loudly and strikes his breast to declare himself a sinner, and then he invokes the intercession of a variety of apostles and martyrs, including some female sainted martyrs (Felicitas, Perpetua, Agatha, Lucy, Cecilia, and Anastasia) in expression of our hope that someday we might join them in heaven.

---

5 The word *peccatoribus* means "sinners." It is the striking of the breast that actually touches upon those muscles of the chest.

33. Per Quem Haec Omnia

The last location in the family room is the door on the way out (33), and here you'll recall we saw a queen proclaiming *"Hey, come near!"* The Per Quem Haec Omnia begins, as you might expect by now, with the works, *"Per Quem Haec Omnia"* and continues *"Domine, semper bona creas, sancti+ficas, vivi+ficas, bene+dicis, et praestas nobis."* ("By whom, O Lord, Thou dost always create, sanctify +, quicken +, bless +, and bestow upon us all these good things.") If you'd like, you can imagine a Dachshund dog at her side, because this pray precedes the Final Doxology. The priest now uncovers the chalice and genuflects. Rising he grasps the Host in his right hand and the chalice in his left, performs the Sign of the Cross a full five times above the chalice as he recites *"Per Ipsum, Et Cum Ip+so, Et In Ip+so, est tibi Deo Patri + omnipotenti, in unitate Spiritus + Sancti, omnis honor, et gloria"* ("Through Him +, And

With Him +, and In Him + is unto Thee, God the Father + Almighty, in the unity of the Holy + Ghost, all honor and glory.") The priest then lays down the host, covers the chalice, genuflects, and says:

Priest: *Per omnia saecula saeculorum.* (World without end.)

Server: *Amen.*

So end the prayers of the Canon. We rise, and the priest recites that familiar prayer taught to his apostles by Jesus Christ Himself. The Communion Rite has begun and we'll write it on the tablets of our hearts in the very next chapter. In the meanwhile, do you know the parts of the Canon? If not, let's look at the table and pictures until we know backward and forward all ten of its silent blasts.

PART 5

COMMUNION RITES

Facing the people with the Ciborium and holding up one of the Sacred Particles before the communicants the priest says:

Behold the Lamb of God: behold Him Who taketh away the sins of the world.

He then repeats the Domine non sum dignus three times as before his own communion, and going to the Communion rail places a consecrated Host in the mouth of the each communicant, saying at the same time:

May the Body of Our Lord Jesus Christ keep thy soul unto life everlasting. Amen.

Fr. Lasance[1]

We now enter a room of this house not only with a "cathedral ceiling," but, indeed, an entire cathedral! At the rear of the cathedral,

---

1 *The New Roman Missal*, 98.

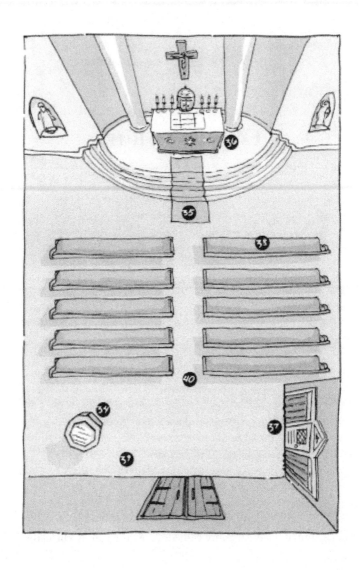

right next to the baptismal font (location 34), believe it or not, you see a *potter* with his *nose* in a *toaster*. You can tell he is a potter by the clay on his hands. That toast must have just smelled a little too good, and now unfortunately, his nose is stuck. On next to the center aisle front (35), just before the steps to the altar, you see a famous *liberal* politician of your choice who says that he *knows* and then proceeds to *quiz us*. Next, at the site of the altar itself (36) you see a woman named *Agnes* holding up a very strange calendar with a big "X" on *"Day E."* Moving along to the confessional booth at the rear right (37) you *kneel in prayer*, your eyes fixated on a large *host* that is floating in front of the door. Stopping next (and the last time for this chapter), at the front right pew (38), you see *your priest consuming two halves of a host.*

That completes our memory tour for this chapter, and indeed we are only five locations from the end of our tour of this memory house housing the Traditional Latin Mass. Do you have them all backwards and forwards, inside and out: (34) at the font with the potter's nose in the toaster, (35) center front with the liberal who knows and quizzes us, (36) the altar with Agnes and her calendar's "Day E," (37) the confessional where you kneel in prayer before a host, and finally (38) the right front pew with your priest consuming two halves of a host? Sure you do! (If not, let's rehearse one more time.) Now that you've got it all, let's zoom in to see just what you have got.

34. Baptismal font	*Potter's nose in toaster*	Pater Noster (Our Father)

35. Center front	*Liberal knows/quizzes us*	Libera Nos Quaesumus
36. Altar	*Agnus' calender shows Day E*	Agnus Dei
37. Confessional	*Kneeling in prayer before host*	Prayers before Communion
38. Front pew right	*Priest receives two halves of host*	Communion

34. Pater Noster

How odd that within the baptismal font (34) we found a potter's nose stuck in a toaster. "Potter's nose, toaster" will serve to remind us through its sounds of the *Pater Noster*. To lock in the meaning of this image too, simply have the potter praying the Our Father! *Pater Noster*, of course, is Latin for *Our Father*. The *Pater Noster* is also known as the Lord's Prayer since Jesus taught it (Matt. 6:11-19; Luke 11:2-4). This prayer has been part of the Mass from the early centuries of the Church. You already know the English words. For now I'll present this prayer in Latin as it is said in the Mass (a beautiful and euphonious prayer well worth memorizing!)

First, the priest begins: *Oremus.* (Let us pray.)

Praeceptis saluatribus moniti, et divina institutione formati, audemus dicere:

(Admonished by Thy saving precepts and following thy divine instruction, we make bold to say:)

Pater Noster, qui es in caelis: Sanctificetur nomen tuum: Adveniat regnum tuum: Fiat voluntas tua, sicut in caelo, et in terra. Panem nostrum quotidianum da nobis hodie: Et dimmite nobis debita nostra, sicut et nos dimittimus debitoribus nostris. Et ne nos inducas in tentationem.

Server: *Sed libera nos a malo.*

Priest: *Amen.*

35. Libera Nos Quaesumus

At the center aisle of the church, before the altar steps (35), we saw a famous liberal politician (of your choice) who said he knows something and then proceed to quiz us. "Liberal, knows, quiz us" will serve to remind us of *Libera Nos Quaesumus,* the prayer that follows and elaborate upon the last words of the *Pater Noster.* The Latin word *libera* here derives from their word for "freedom," *nos* means "us," and *quaesumus* means "'to vouchsafe or give graciously." This prayer begins *"Libera nos quaesumus, Domine, ab omnibus malis…"* ("Deliver us, Lord, we pray, from every evil…) As he recites this prayer, the priest holds the paten between his first and second fingers. The prayer includes a call for the intercession of the Virgin Mary, Mother of God, the Apostles Peter and Paul, as well as Andrew (Peter's younger brother) and all the saints, beseeching God that he might grant peace, help, mercy, freedom free sin and from insecurity.

The priest then uncovers the chalice, genuflects, and taking the host, breaks it in two pieces above the chalice praying *"Per eundem Dominum nostrum Jesum Christum Filium tuum…"* ("Through the same Jesus Christ, Thy Son our Lord…") He then breaks off a particle from the divided Host, saying, *"Qui tecum vivit et regnat in unitate Spiritus Sancti Deus",* ("Who liveth and reigneth with Thee in the unity of the Holy Ghost, God.") Then he prays, *"Per omnia saecula saeculorum"* ("World without end") to which the server responds, *"Amen."*

Now, the priest makes the Sign of the Cross over the chalice and says: *"Pax + Domini sit + semper vobis + cum"* ("May the peace + of the Lord be + always + with you.") The server responds, *"Et cum spiritu tuo"* ("And with thy spirit.") The priest then places the particle of the Host in the chalice, saying quietly, *"Haec commixtio, et consecratio Corporis et Sanguinis Domini nostri Jesu Christi, fiat accipientibus nobis in vitam aeternam. Amen."* ("May this mingling and hallowing of the Body and Blood of our Lord Jesus Christ be for us who receive it a source of eternal life. Amen.")

As to why the Body and Blood of Christ are mingled, Dom Gueranger notes that the rite goes back over one thousand years and offers this interpretation of its meaning in words well worth pondering for how they remind us of just how intimately the Mass re-presents Christ's own sacrifice and triumph for us:

> Its object is to show, that, at the moment of our Lord's Resurrection, His Blood was reunited to His Body, by flowing again in His veins as before. It would not have sufficed if His soul alone had been reunited to His Body: His Blood must necessarily be so likewise, in order that the Lord might be whole and complete. Our Saviour, therefore, when rising, took back His Blood which was erstwhile spilled on Calvary, in the Praetorium, and in the Garden of Olives.[2]

36. Agnus Dei

Now you'll recall that upon the altar (36) we saw a woman named Agnes with an odd calendar upon to a page showing "Day E." "Agnes, Day E," should serve pretty well to remind us of the *Agnus Dei*, and if you'd like to easily lock in the meaning as well, just have Agnes holding a lamb.[3]

The priest covers the chalice, genuflects, then bows and strikes his breast three times in repentance of his sins. He then prays, recalling

---

2 Dom Prosper Gueranger, O.S.B., *Explanation of the Holy Mass*, 184.

3 My own parish is named in honor of St. Agnes. This early martyr (c.291 –c. 304) is usually depicted holding a lamb in her arms. *Agnus* is the Latin word for lamb.

the words of St. John the Baptist[4]: *"Agnus Dei, qui tollis peccata mundi: misere nobis. Agnus Dei, qui tollis peccata mundi: misere nobis. Agnus Dei, qui tollis peccata munid: dona nobis pacem."* (Lamb of God, Who takest away the sins of the world, have mercy on us. Lamb of God, Who takest away the sins of the word, have mercy on us. Lamb of God, Who takest away the sins of the world, grant us peace.") Here we pray that the holy Eucharist will unite us all in peace.

37. Prayers before Communion

Our next stop in the mnemonic cathedral was the confession box (37), and as we knelt in prayer to our surprise our eyes were riveted by a large host floating in the air in front of the doors. This image should remind us of the prayers before communion. The priest directs his eyes toward the Sacrament, and not kneeling, but bowing, begins the first of three silent prayers. The first begins *"Domine Jesu Christe, qui dixti Apostolis tuis: Pacem relinquo vobis, pacem meam do vobis…"* ("O Lord, Jesus Christ, Who didst say to Thine Apostles: Peace I leave you, My peace I give you.") The remainder of this prayer asks God for peace and unity. The priest then continues with a second silent prayer for holiness directed to the Holy Trinity, beginning, *"Domine Jesu Christe, Fili Dei vivi…"* ("O Lord Jesus Christ, Son of the living God…") In his last of three prayers before his own Communion, the priest continues silently a prayer for grace, beginning *"Perceptio Corporis tui,*

---

4 The next day he saw Jesus coming toward him and said, "Behold the Lamb of God, who takes away the sins of the world" (John 1:29).

Domine Jesu Christe, quod ego indignus sumere praesumo…" ("Let not the partaking of Thy Body, O Lord Jesus Christ, which I, though unworthy, presume to receive…"), and ending *"Qui vivis et regnas cum Deo Patre in unitate Spiritus Sancti Deus, per omnia saecula saeculorum. Amen."* ("Who livest and reignest with God the Father, in the unity of the Holy Ghost, God, world without end. Amen.")

38. Communion

In the last location of this chapter's memory tour, we saw at the right front pew (38) your own priest giving himself communion, receiving two halves of the host. This is because after the third of the Pre-Communion prayers, the priest then genuflects, takes the host and says prayers beginning with *"Panem caelestem accipiam, et nomen Domini invocabo."* ("I will take the Bread of Heaven, and will call upon the Name of the Lord.") Striking his breast he utters those words recalling the centurion: *"Domine non sum dignus, ut inters sub tectum meum: sed tantum dic verbo, et sanabitur anima mea."* ("Lord, I am not worthy that Thou shouldst enter under my roof; but only say the word, and my soul shall be healed.") The bells are rung three times at the start of this prayer and the priest repeats it three times. The priest then makes the Sign of the Cross over the paten, prays that the Body of Christ will give him everlasting life, and receives both halves of the host. He continues in silent prayers, praising and thanking God. Making the Sign of the Cross, while holding the chalice, he prays: *"Sanguis Domini nostril Jesu Christi custodiat animam meam in vitam aeternam. Amen."* ("May the Blood of Our Lord Jesus Christ preserve my soul unto everlasting life. Amen.") He then receives the Precious Blood of Christ.

The server then says the *Confiteor* (we encountered at location 2), and then the priest turns to the people and says, *"Misereatur vestri omnipotens Deus, et dismissis peccatis vestris, perducat vos ad vitam aeternam."* ("May Almighty God have mercy on you, forgive your sins, and bring you to everlasting life." The server answers *"Amen."* The priest then recites prayers in Latin that begin *"Ecce Agnus Dei…"* ("Behold the Lamb of God…") and *"Domine, non sum dignus…"* ("Lord, I am not worthy…"). Bells are rung three times before the *"Domine, non sum dignus…"* and again, the priest recites this prayer three times.

And now it is time for us to receive the Lord Jesus Christ in Communion. The communicants proceed to the front of the church and kneel upon the altar rail. (In some churches without an altar rail the front pew may be used.) While the communicants are kneeling, hands folded in prayer, the priest says *"Corpus Domini nostri Jesu Christi custodiat animam tuam in vitam aeternam. Amen."* ("May the Body of Our Lord Jesus Christ preserve your soul unto life everlasting. Amen.") The priest places the host on our tongue, and we do not answer "Amen," but return to our pew in thankful prayer.

When all have received Communion, the priest returns to the altar, drinks wine poured into the chalice and says prayers of thanksgiving, beginning *"Quod ore sumpsimus, Domine, pura mente capiamus: et de munere temporali fiat nobis remedium semptiernum."* ("Grant, O Lord, that what we have taken with our mouth, we may receive with a pure mind; and that from a temporal gift it may become for us an everlasting remedy.") The rite of *ablutions* (cleansing) follows. Wine and water are poured into the chalice over the priest's fingers as he prays silently that Christ's Body and Blood that he has received will *"adhaeret visceribus meis,"* ("cleave to my innermost parts") removing any remaining stains of sins, refreshed by the holy Sacraments.

It would serve us to meditate upon the fact that we too have received Christ into our own viscera, our "innermost parts." Will we then do our part to show our gratitude in our actions for such a grand benefit?

The priest then recites a Communion verse from the epistle side of the altar (the right from our perspective.) This prayer is a changing proper. The example from the Coalition in Support of Ecclesia Dei's, *Latin-English Booklet Missal* for the Mass of Holy Trinity Sunday is as follows:

> *Benedicimus Deum caeli, et coram omnibus viventibus confitebimur ei: quia fecit nobiscum misericordiam suam.*

> We bless the God of Heaven, and before all the living we will praise Him; because He hath shown His mercy to us.

> Then from the middle of the altar is proclaimed.

> Priest: *Dominus vobiscum.* (The Lord be with you.)

> Server: *Et cum spiritu tuo.* (And with thy spirit.)

> Priest: *Oremus.* (Let us pray.)

The prayer that then follows prepares us for the conclusion of the Mass and takes us into our last chapter. At this point, however, I pray that you do tell if you have memorized this chapter's five main parts of the Latin Mass, from the *Pater Noster* (34) to the *Libera Nos Quesumas* (35), to the *Agnes Dei* (36), to the Prayers Before Communion (37), to the Communion Rites (38)? If not, it is time to rehearse them. If so, it is time to meditate deeply upon their meanings and to experience them when you next have a chance to participate in the holy sacrifice of the Mass.

— PART 6 —

POST-COMMUNION RITES

It must surprise a stranger that, after we have solemnly told the people to go away, they stay and the service continues. The explanation, of course, is that the three elements after "Ite missa est," the Placeat Prayer, blessing, and last gospel, are all late additions....The Last Gospel is one of the latest additions to the Mass. The beginning of St. John's Gospel (i, 1-14) was the object of special devotion from the time of the Fathers. St. Augustine tells of a man who wanted this to be written in letters of gold in every church.

Fr. Adrian Fortescue[1]

On we go now to the back of our church (39), where you see near a *stamped envelope* with the word *"Communion"* written on it. At the start of the center aisle (40), there stands not a bride getting ready

---

1 Adrian Fortescue, *The Mass: A Study of Roman Liturgy* (Middletown, DE: First Rate Publishers, 2015), ch. 10, section 3, pages not numbered. Fr. Fortescue's book was originally published in 1912.

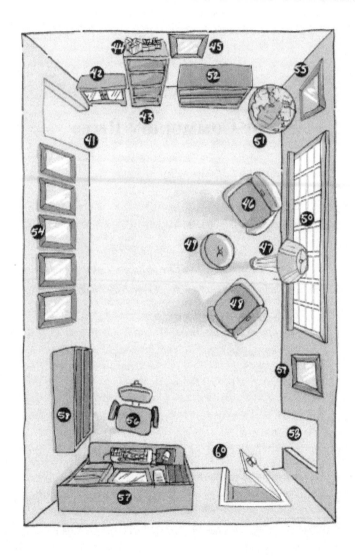

to go forth, but a Japanese person, encouraging her friend Esther to eat some miso soup. You hear her say, *"Eat a miso, Est."* Now we move into our very last room where we need barely step inside to complete our whole memory tour of the Mass. You arrive at the door of a study (41), and on it is a sign with an *old Irish blessing.*[2] Last, but certainly not least, sitting atop a small bookshelf just inside the door (42) is our familiar *"Good Newsboy"* proclaiming the best of news for the very *last* time.

Have you written this last batch of images on the tablet of your heart? If so, congratulations! You have mastered the key parts of the Traditional Latin Mass! This memory tour has ended. Go in peace to love and serve the Lord – but ideally not until you've considered the awesome significance of these last four rites of the Mass.

39. Back of church	*Envelope stamped "Communion"*	Post-communion
40. Start of center aisle	*"Eat a miso, Est."*	Ite Missa Est
41. Study door	*Irish blessing posted on door*	The Blessing
42. Short bookcase	*The last "Good News" boy*	The Last Gospel

---

2 I suggest this one: "May the road rise to meet you. May the wind be ever at your back. May the sun shine warm upon your face, and the rain fall soft upon your fields. And until we meet again, may God hold you in the palm of His hand." (You don't necessarily have to memorize it. Just enjoy it!)

39. Post-communion

We saw at the back of the memory church (39), an envelope stamped with the word "Communion." This image will remind us of the *Post-communion* rites. The priest begins with a changing, proper prayer, such as this example, beginning with *"Proficiat nobis ad salutem corporis et animae, Domine Deus noster, hujus sacramenti susceptio; et sempiternae sanctae Trinitatis, ejusdemque individuae unitatis confessio."* (May the reception of this Sacrament, O Lord our God, and the confession of the holy and eternal Trinity and of its undivided Unity, profit us to the salvation of body and soul...") The remainder of the prayer is the familiar phrasing declaring that this be through Jesus Christ in unity with the Holy Spirit, God for ever and ever, ending in *"Amen."*

40. Ite Missa Est

Back at the start of the nave's central aisle (40), we found that Japanese woman inviting her friend Esther to eat some miso soup, hoping that her English words "Eat a miso, Est!" would remind us of the important Latin words, *"Ite Missa Est."* Having reminded us of the Communion we have just received, in the Post-communion Prayer, the priest goes to the center of the altar, kisses it, turns to the people and says out loud:

Priest: *Dominus vobiscum.* (The Lord be with you.)

Server: *Et cum spiritu tuo.* (And with thy spirit.)

Priest: *Ite, Missa est.* (Go, the Mass is ended.)

Server: *Deo gratias.* (Thanks be to God.)

This is the "Dismmal" and it is from the word *"Missa"* in it that that Mass took its name. Still, at certain times, such as Lent, the *"Ite, Missa est"* is omitted and the priest instead faces the altar and says, *"Benedicamus Domino"* ("Let us bless the Lord") and the server responds *"Deo gratias."* ("Thanks be to God.") Dom Gueranger notes that it was expected that during the season of Lent, the people would not leave the church right after Mass, but would stay for a time of additional prayer.

41. The Blessing

We just started to dip into the study, and upon the entrance door (41) we saw that plaque with an old Irish blessing. The blessing here though is not Irish but Latin. The priest bows before the altar and silently prays a blessing beginning *"Placeat Tibi, Sancta Trinitas obsequium*

servitutis meae…" (May the tribute of my homage be pleasing to Thee, O most holy Trinity…") The priest prays that the Mass be acceptable to God and bring forgiveness to him and to all for whom the Mass was offered, *"per Christum Dominum nostrum. Amen"* (through Christ our Lord. Amen.")

The priest then kisses the altar and turns toward the people bestowing the Final Blessing:

Priest: *Benedicat Vos Omnipotens Deus, Pater, et Filius, + et Spiritus Sanctus.*

May Almighty God Bless You; the Father, the Son + and the Holy Ghost.

Server: *Amen.*

Dom Gueranger relates that because this blessing is a sign of joy, it is not included in *Requiem* (funeral) Masses.

42. The Last Gospel

At the last location of this memory house, sitting atop a small bookcase (42), was, for the last time, our familiar *"Good newsboy."* We know well by now from past mnemonic experience, that the good news he proclaims is always the Gospel of our Lord Jesus Christ. This time though, the same Gospel message is proclaimed at the end of every Mass. The Last Gospel begins, *"In Principio erat Verbum, et Verbum erat apud Deum…"* ("In the Beginning was the Word, and the Word was with God, and the Word was God.") This is the first verse of St. John's Gospel which makes crystal clear in the loftiest of words, that the Lord Jesus Christ, about Whom he will tell us, was the Word (with a capital W) and verily God Himself. The reading proceeds through the end of the 13th verse, whereupon all genuflect as the priest declares from verse 14, *"ET VERBO CARO FACTUM EST,"* (AND THE WORD WAS MADE FLESH") and (in translation) "and dwelt among us, and we saw His glory, the glory as of the Only-begotten of the Father, full of grace and truth." The server responds *"Deo gratias…"* ("Thanks be to God.")

How beautiful and moving that since the Middle Ages, when the Catholics of the time were so profoundly stirred by the words of the Word in this Gospel, that the Latin Mass unto our time ends with this most sublime of Gospel passages.

This then, formally ends the Traditional Latin Mass, and yet when you attend such a Mass you will likely see that it is still not quite yet time to go home. Though it was omitted from the 1962 Missal, Latin Masses will often conclude with the priest and congregation (while kneeling) praying in English the Hail Mary three times, the Hail Holy Queen, the prayer beginning, "O God, Our Refuge And Our Strength" (staring with the first verses of Psalm 46 [45] and adding calls for the intercessions of Mother Mary and all the saints), and finally the prayer to Saint Michael the Archangel.[3]

There then, we have completed the entire memory tour of the

---

3 Pope Leo XIII added this prayer to the end of the Low Mass in 1886. In my diocese of Springfield, IL, Bishop Thomas John Paprocki returned this prayer to the end of the Mass several years ago.

Traditional Latin or Tridentine Mass. Do you have these last four parts down pat now, from the Post-communion (39) to the *Ita Missa Est* (40), to the Final Blessing (41), and last, but far from least, the Last Gospel (42)? If not, you know by now that it simply means it is time for a bit more rehearsal. When you have them all down, why not set aside a minute for prayer to thank God and his Church for such a wonderful gift as our Traditional Roman Rite of the Mass. And then we'll move on to conclude with some thoughts on how we can more fully participate in the Holy Sacrifice of the Mass, indeed, as if our life depended on it (because in a way, it sure does).

— PART 7 —

CONCLUSION: FULL PARTICIPATION AT MASS IN HEART, MIND, BODY, AND SOUL

You shall love the Lord, your God, with all your heart, with all your soul, and with all your mind.

Matthew 22:37

Glorify God in your body.

1 Cor. 6:20

Christ has called us to love God with all that we are, to give to Him all that we have to give. All that we have to give, our very existence itself, is of course a gift from God in the first place. He gives us his loving Holy Spirit too and his Son Incarnate, nowhere this side of heaven with such an immediate and intimate presence as at the Holy

Sacrifice of the Mass. Christ gives Himself to us in his holy Word, and in his Body and Blood, Soul, and Divinity. Christ is truly present to us at every Mass. As we sit, and kneel, and stand in the pews are we truly present to Him?

We are urged to actively participate in the Mass, in our physical presence and bodily actions, and in our hearts and minds, too. Having worked to memorize the parts of the Mass, what can we do to become more present to Christ and to participate with Him more full at every Mass we attend? Christ and His apostles have already advised us how to do so, by loving God with all that we are, in heart, mind, body, and soul.

Heart

The heart is at the heart of this book, since our goal has most clearly been to write the rites of the Mass upon the tablets of our hearts. Only important things are worth the concerted, repeated efforts of learning them by heart, and here the Mass more than qualifies. Important things are things that we cherish the most, things that affect the *core* of our being, recalling the Latin word for heart is in fact the word *cor,* and that metaphorically speaking, the heart is also the seat of love. When we make the repeated efforts to memorize the Mass, we demonstrate to God that the Son and His Mass are truly most dear to our hearts.

Mind

God made us in his image and likeness with intellect and will. Indeed, St. Augustine wrote that the three parts of the soul of *memory*, *understanding,* and *will* parallel within us the three persons of the Holy Trinity. God gave us minds or intellects capable of understanding in a manner far exceeding any other species on earth, and he expects us to use them, even, and perhaps especially at Mass. Truly the Mass is a mystery that exceeds our capacity to ever *fully* understand it, but Christ Himself has called us to love God with *all* of our mind. It is incumbent then on us to attempt to grow in the understanding of the Mass within the limits of our own mental powers. We will never begin to know those limits unless we strive to test them.

Let's think of that hour or so that we spend in the Mass. Do the parts of the Mass zoom by us one by one with only a vague sense of where we've been so far and what yet remains? Should we not rather strive to have an overarching understanding of the Mass's structure and sequence? Many of us move through Mass like the person who travels alone along an unfamiliar hilly road, never knowing for sure what lies beyond the next hill, when we could have the perspective of one who views the scene from above with a bird's-eye view, seeing the whole route and sequence of the Mass all at once, and grasping thereby how the all the parts relate to each other like a great, holy symphony.[1]

We use the reasoning and imaginative powers of our minds even as we memorize the Mass, for the memory methods we employ were

---

1 St. Thomas Aquinas, by the way, provides this metaphor for God's knowledge of *all* things at *all* times from the perspective of eternity: "Just as he who goes along the road, does not see all who come after him; whereas he who sees the whole road from a height, sees at once all travelling by the way." (*Summa Theologica,* I. Q. 14, a. 13.)

invented through human reason and cannot operate within us without a great deal of thought and attention at first, until they become deeply ingrained and virtually automatic. Of course, since we seek not merely to *memorize* names and sequences of rites but to *understand* them as deeply as we are able, when we set this book aside, we will also pick up other books, the Scriptures themselves and other books on the Mass, books by great saints of all ages and by modern writers of our time who can take us ever deeper into the origins, development, and meaning of each and every part of the Mass, through the Scriptures and the Tradition of the Holy Catholic Church.[2]

Hopefully, you have already begun to see as well that the very memory exercises within this book are a veritable workout for your mind as well. Decades of medical and psychological research have shown that to retain as best as possible one's mental powers of thinking, reasoning, and remembering as one ages, the golden rules that has emerged is simply "use it or lose it." Memory training is one way we can become stewards of the intellects God has graced us with, aiding us in maintaining the mental faculties God has given us as we inch closer to the likes of Methuselah.

Younger people too can profit through memory training in their abilities to love God with their minds. In our world of overwhelming

---

2 The footnotes in this book can give you a start since I have cited many, though not all, of the excellent books on the Mass that I pulled from the great big box of dozens of books that has sat by my side throughout these months of writing.

technology, many assume they need not memorize anything since the phone in their pocket seems to hold every answer to every possible question. Need the sequence of the rites of the Mass? Why not just do an Internet search? What a world of difference there is though from having the Mass accessible to you in an electronic gadget from having it written in the tablet of your own heart. When the Mass is in your heart and mind it can change lives for the better in a way all the electronic devices in your pocket or in the whole world can never begin to do.

That electronic world also provides us with a world of distractions, with temptations toward what medieval theologians called the vice of *"curiositas,"* that is of excessive caring and concern about things that do not matter. We see it today in electronic "addictions" for things like social media and Internet surfing, texting, and email checking, where people seem driven to spend hours at a time, searching, skimming, clicking, and keyboarding, each new message or image titillating, but never satisfying, and so very little worth resting upon and thoroughly digesting. These memory methods can help train us in the contrary virtue of *"studiositas"* (studiousness), which is the ability to focus and think calmly and deeply on the things that truly matter the most – like the Holy Mass.[3]

---

3 See St. Thomas Aquinas's *Summa Theologica*, II-II, Q. 166 for his detailed treatment of the virtue of studiousness.

Body

God made us beings with bodies and souls, and our bodies are not unimportant.

We are to glorify God in our bodies, by keeping our bodies sexually pure and by being good stewards of our God-given bodies through reasonable eating and exercise. Our bodies also serve to glorify God in Holy Sacrifice of the Mass. Outsiders and newcomers to the Catholic Church are often perplexed by the various bodily postures and gestures that accompany the rites of the Mass and even many Catholics do not understand their complete significance. Whether standing at full attention, sitting to absorb Scriptural readings or a sermon, or kneeling in deep reverence during the Eucharistic prayer or at Communion, all of the bodily postures, including bending of the knee in genuflections (*genu* is knee in Latin), bowing, and the repeated Signs of the Cross are the visible demonstrations of our glorification of God at the Holy Mass. We should strive to learn the significance of each and every posture and gesture and to perform them with full understanding and reverence.

Soul

What better place than the Mass than to reflect on the fact that God crafted us as ensouled beings with immaterial and immortal souls that will only attain complete and lasting bliss through the beatific vision of His Godhead in heaven. The Mass is a taste of heaven on earth. Christ makes Himself present, with the angels and saints at his attendance. It is up to us to what extent we'll let Christ speak to our souls in through the Gospels and in to come and dwell and to cleave "within our innermost parts" in the Eucharist.

Admiral Denton, a prisoner on earth, called his time in prison a session in hell, and yet he was able to endure that hell year after year by his daily visits to heaven during which he mentally recited to himself the Mass, both in Latin and in its English translation. May we learn from the admiral's admiral lesson what a thing worth cherishing is the holy and heavenly Mass. May we learn from the great Saints Albert and Thomas Aquinas how we too can write the script of heavenly worship on the tablets of our hearts.

May we then strive to love God with all our heart, mind, body, and soul as we express to Him the deepest of thanks by memorizing the gift of the Mass, seeking to understand it more deeply, experience it more often, and live it more fully in every day in every act of our lives.

TRADITIONAL LATIN MASS SUMMARY TABLE

LOCATION	*IMAGE*	PART OF MASS
1. Front Door	*David signs cross, says, "Adjudicate me."*	Judica Me
2. Door mat	*Con fits Eeyore*	Confiteor
3. Glass panel next to door	*Cloud of incense*	Incensing the Altar
4. Picture on wall	*Car made in Detroit, faded D*	Introit
5. Gun rack	*Valkyries*	Kyrie
6. Center of foyer	*Singer or friend named Gloria (or "Old Glory")*	Gloria
7. Chandelier	*Collection basket full of prayers*	Collect
8. Mirror	*Pistol with E rests on letter*	Epistle
9. Bench	*Graduate named Al goes up stairs*	Gradual
10. Drawer	*Al and Lulu on train track*	Allelulia or Tract

11. Center of living room	*Giant golden sequins trickle down*	Sequence
12. Picture window	*Newsboy proclaims "Good news!"*	Gospel
13. Sofa	*Fates in nice scene*	Credo
14. Coffee table	*You offer Tory bread and wine*	Offertory
15. Television	*Could of incense rises*	Incensing alter, etc.
16. Fireplace	*Lava bowl for washing hands*	Lavabo
17. Living room doorway	*Sue, Skippy, & Santa eat a Trindad*	Suscipe, Sancta Trinitas
18. Dining room doorway	*Oar, latte, frat brothers*	Orate Fratres
19. Foot of table	*Your priest's face*	Preface
20. Center of table	*Sanka, tusk*	Sanctus
21. Thermometer	*Canon blasts/ "Tea, I get' er."*	Te Igitur
22. Seat on right	*Mnemosyne's toe moves*	Memento of the Living
23. Head of table	*Communists counting*	Communicantes
24. Seat on left	*"Honk, Ich(abod). It's her!"*	Hanc Igitur
25. Door to family room	*Qualms about a monk with O-shaped plate*	Quam Oblationem
26. Dresser	*Priest in awe raises host*	Consecration of the Host
27. Television	*Priest in awe raises chalice*	Consecration of the Wine

28. Closet	*Under Mnemosyne is statue of the Lord*	Unde et Memores
29. Weight bench	*Superman shows proper way*	Supra Quae Propitio
30. Pool table	*Supplies: tea, stroganoff*	Supplices te Rogamus
31. Recliner	*Mnemosyne in casket*	Memento of the Dead
32. Couch	*Nobles quote, "Pec tore a bus!"*	Nobis Quoque Peccatoribus
33. Doorway out	*Per Queen, "Hey, come near!"*	Per Quem Haec Omnia
34. Baptismal font	*Potter's nose in toaster*	Pater Noster (Our Father)
35. Center front	*Liberal knows/quizzes us*	Libera Nos Quae-sumus
36. Altar	*Agnus' calender shows Day E*	Agnus Dei
37. Confessional	*Kneeling in prayer before host*	Prayers before Communion
38. Front pew right	*Priest receives two halves of host*	Communion
39. Back of church	*Envelope stamped "Com-munion"*	Postcommuion
40. Start of center aisle	*"Eat a miso, Est."*	Ite Missa Est
41. Study door	*Irish blessing posted on door*	The Blessing
42. Short bookcase	*The last "Good News" boy*	The Last Gospel

— Appendix B —

Lasting Reflections on the Last Gospel

Vidi Dominum sedentem super solium excelsum et elevatum, et plena erat omnis terra maisestate eius, et ea quae sub ipso errant, replebant templum.

I saw the Lord seated on a high and lofty throne, and the whole house was full of his majesty, and the things that were under him filled the temple.

Isaiah 6:1

In principio erat Verbum, et Verbum erat apud Deum. Et Deus erat Verbum. Hoc erat in principio apud Deum. Omnia per ipsum facta sunt. Et sine ipso factum est nihil. Quod factum est.

In the beginning was the Word, and the Word with was God, and the Word was God. The same was in the beginning with God. All things were made by him; and without him was made nothing that was made.

John 1:1-3

Surprised by John

I must admit that at first I was surprised and intrigued as an adult to find the Last Gospel (John 1:1-14) read at the end of every Latin Mass.[1] Now, I am awed by it and thankful that through the Holy Spirit's stirrings these words of unsurpassed sublimity did become part of the Mass.

Though the words have been cherished and recited as a private devotion since the time of St. John wrote them in the first century, this passage did not become part of the Mass until the middle ages. Priests would recite the verses as part of their prayers after Mass. The *Caeremoniale Episcoporum* that prescribes liturgical guidelines for bishops directed that they start the words of this passage at the altar and continue to it "by heart" as he goes off to take off his vestments. Pope Pius V made the Last Gospel a universal practice for the Roman Rite Missal in 1570.[2]

The Prophet, the Eagle, the Angelic Doctor, the Thomist, and the Scientist

Happily for us who have come to love the Last Gospel and the wisdom of St. Thomas Aquinas, among the most thorough and sublime of St. Thomas Aquinas's scriptural commentaries is his *Commen-*

---

1 With a few exceptions, such as Christmas Day in which John 1:1-14 is that day's Gospel reading for the Mass.

2 For historical details see the Gospel in the Liturgy entry in the New Advent Catholic Encyclopedia at http://www.newadvent.org/cathen/06659a.htm.

tary on the Gospel of John. Indeed, his comments on the fourteen verses that comprise the Last Gospel take up about 65 pages! And even beyond that, St. Thomas precedes his discussion with two prologues on John's Gospel, the second one on St. Jerome's comments on the Gospel, and the first one on the verse from the prophet Isaiah that was cited at the start of this appendix. St. Thomas notes that the words of Isaiah's vision could indeed have been spoken by St. John the Evangelist, so well do they reflect that heights of contemplation he shared in his gospel.

To repeat the words of the prophet:

"I saw the Lord seated on a high throne, and the whole house was full of his majesty, and the things that were under him filled the temple." (Isaiah 6:1).

St. Thomas reflects:

"These are the words of a contemplative, and if we regard them as spoken by John the Evangelist they apply quite well in show-ing the nature of this Gospel."[3]

Further:

"The contemplation of John is described above in three ways, in keeping with the threefold manner in which he contemplated the Lord Jesus. It is described as high, full, and perfect. It is high: *I saw the Lord seated on a high and lofty throne*; it is full; *and the whole*

---

3 St. Thomas Aquinas, *Commentary on the Gospel of John* (chapters 1 – 8), (Lander, WY: The Aquinas Institute for the Study of Sacred Doctrine, 2013), 1.

house was full of his majesty; and it was perfect; *and the things that were under him filled the temple."*[4]

Unlike the gospels of Sts. Matthew, Mark, and Luke which start with the story of Jesus as *man* and then reveal Him as *God*, St. John's Gospel starts at the top, so to speak, declaring boldly in its very first words that Jesus Christ always was and is eternally the Word of God, God Himself, and with God, who became Incarnate in time in this world to enlighten and save us. This is part of the reason St. John has traditionally been depicted as an eagle, a bird that soars high and can look at the sun.

The 20th century Thomist Fr. Réginald Garrigou-Lagrange, O.P., made similar observations on the Gospel of St. John while reflecting on the Holy Spirit's gifts of knowledge and wisdom. While the gift of knowledge judges primarily of lower, earthly, and human things, it can move us toward the consideration of the higher things of God, but only indirectly, considering how these earthly effects derive from higher causes. "The gift of wisdom," on the other hand, per Fr.Garrigou-Lagrange, "proceeds in the opposite direction. It judges first of divine things, then of created things as insets of the divine." Indeed, he observes that the Gospel of St. Matthew may be seen to follow the path of the gift of knowledge in preaching Christ, starting with Christ's human genealogy and rising from the things of the earth to the things of heaven, while St. John's Gospel, starts straight off with Christ as "the Word" in the first verse, "portraying in the higher light

---

4 Ibid.

of wisdom that radiates from above, out through the lower streams of knowledge, with which St. Matthew is more conversant."[5]

There is an interesting anecdote regarding the last gospel in the life of St. Thomas's great teacher, St. Albert the Great, the patron saint of scientists, and also a memory master. In the year 1254, a Bavarian member of a regular religious order received a vision while praying at St. Peter's in Rome. A monstrous serpent had writhed into the basilica, with horrible hissing that filled not only the church but all of Rome. Just then a man arrived, clothed in the habit of the Order of Preachers, whose name was revealed to him as Albert. The serpent attacked Albert, encircling him head to toe in its muscular, slithering coils. The friar burst free, though, and made his way to the pulpit, whereupon he read from the Gospel of St. John up to the words *"Verbum caro factum est et habitavit in nobis"* "And the Word became flesh and dwelled among us," 1:14." (Sound familiar?) At these words the serpent fled and ceased its hissing. When our great Dominican arrived in Rome that same year, the man told Albert of his vision, but Albert could not discern its meaning.

Two years later in 1256, Pope Alexander IV summoned Albert to Anagni, the seat of the papacy at the time. It seems certain secular teachers from the University of Paris had been spreading venomous stories about Dominicans and Franciscans of the university. St. Albert responded to their challenge and eventually sent the detractors slithering out of town. The pope was so impressed with Albert's

---

5 Fr. Reginald Garrigou-LaGrange, *The Theological Virtues, Vol. 1 On Faith* (Freiburg: Herder, 1965), 396.

learning and eloquence that he retained him to preach to the papal court about the Gospel of St. John—"*Verbum caro factum est et habitavit in nobis*," and more![6]

Now, St. Albert was not only a champion of his religious order, and of scientific investigation, but of the art of memory as well. Indeed, in his treatise *De Bono* (On the Good), he addressed memory as a part of the virtue of prudence, commented line by line on the *Ad Herennium,* the oldest extant book on the method of loci memory technique, from around 80 BC, and strongly endorsed training in its methods.[7]

So, with the Gospel of St. John still in mind, let's apply the memory methods of Albert and Thomas, the patron saint of scientists and the patron saint of scholars, to that gospel itself, using St. Albert himself as our guide.

Albert's Art of Memory in *Your* Memory Today

Imagine, if you will, that at some time in the future, up in heaven (the good Lord willing), you've asked St. Albert the Great himself if he'd mind guiding you through his favorite Gothic cathedral, fresh in all its newly built glory. The kindly learned man, vibrant like never before in his glorified body and pristine white habit, guides you to a massive *front door* (location 1) of solid gold, and engraved upon it

---

6 See chapter 15 of my *St. Albert the Great: Champion of Faith and Reason* (Charlotte, NC: TAN Books, 2011) for details on this episode.

7 See Mary Carruthers, *The Book of Memory: A Study of Memory in Medieval Culture* (Cambridge: Cambridge University Press, 1990), 267-280 for an English translation of St. Albert's complete commentary.

there you see, not a crucifix or a scene from the Bible or from the lives of the saints, but a massive *Webster's Dictionary*. (Don't worry, I'll tell you why a little later.)

Moving along inside into the narthex (*entranceway* or foyer), (2), St. Albert gently grasps your elbow, guiding you around a *giant flask* sitting on the floor, full to the brim with the most delicious looking deep *red wine* that you have ever seen. Passing through an inner door, you turn to your left to dip your hand in the *holy water basin*, (3) only to find, to your surprise, that someone is bathing *a baby* in there! Moving right along, you sit down in the *left rear pew*, (4) moving past a *woman in unfamiliar exotic clothing*, and you note with a start a deep hole right next to you on the other side. Surrounded by stone with a bucket on its edge, you surmise that it is an ancient *water well*.

Next, looking up toward the front of the church at the *lectern* on the left (5), you see that it is covered, like a *porch*, and stands completely surrounded by a shallow *pool* of water. Glancing up toward the *tabernacle* (6), you see St. Albert himself open it up, revealing not hosts, but *bread* and *fish* (five loaves and two fish to be exact). And there in all His splendor, standing behind the altar (7) is *Jesus Himself*, teaching the congregation. You spy as well, sitting on the altar, an amazing *model replica of the Jewish Temple* of Jerusalem.

Turning next to the wall on the right, you see a *woman* fleeing into the safety of a *confessional booth* (8) as *flying stones* smash against the door. As disturbing as that scene was, you are comforted next as you turn your attention to a magnificent *stained glass window* on the right wall of the cathedral (9). It depicts a *blind man seeing*, and you can see the sun's rays beaming through his eyes. Last, but not least, your attention is drawn to the back right corner of the cathedral (10) by the braying of sheep! And there you see a kindly *shepherd*, leaning on his staff, as his *sheep* quench their thirst in the *baptismal font*.

Do you have all that? If not, please read it through one more time or just look at this handy summary table.

Location	Image
1. Front door	*Dictionary*
2. Entranceway	*Wine flask*
3. Holy water basin	*Baby*
4. Left back pew	*Well*
5. Lectern	*Covered Porch and Pool*
6. Tabernacle	*Bread & Fish*
7. Altar	*Jesus Himself and Temple model*
8. Confessional booth	*Woman fleeing stones*
9. Stained glass window	*Blind man seeing*
10. Baptismal font	*Shepherd watering sheep*

Now let's take a look at what you've *really* committed to memory.

Location (Chapter # from St. John's Gospel)	Image	Gospel Lesson

1. Front door	*Dictionary*	"In the beginning was the Word, and the Word was with God, and the Word was God." (John 10:11.)
2. Entranceway	*Wine flask*	Jesus turns water to wine.
3. Holy water basin	*Baby*	"Unless one is born anew, he cannot see the kingdom of God." (John 3:3.)
4. Left back pew	*Woman and well*	Jesus meets Samaritan woman at Jacob's well.
5. Lectern	*Covered porch and pool*	Jesus heals the paralyzed man at the pool.
6. Tabernacle	*Bread & fish*	Jesus multiples the loaves and fishes.
7. Altar	*Jesus Himself and temple model*	Jesus teaches at the Temple.
8. Confessional booth	*Woman fleeing stones*	Jesus forgives the adulteress.
9. Stained glass window	*Blind man seeing*	Jesus gives the blind man sight.
10. Baptismal font	*Shepherd watering sheep*	"I am the good shepherd. The good shepherd lays down his life for his sheep." (John 10:11.)

Do you see now that those odd and quirky images really served the purpose to remind us of things much more profound? The dictionary should remind us of "The Word," not literal words, but Jesus Christ Himself. So, too, with all the images. The wine flask reminds us of Christ's first miracle, turning water to wine at the wedding feast at Cana, at the request of his Blessed Mother. The baby reminds us we must be "born anew... of the water and the Spirit." (John 3:3,5). The well reminds us how Jesus revealed himself as Christ to the woman from Samaria, since he came to redeem not only the Jews. The porch and the pool remind us of Jesus' miracle of healing the paralyzed man at the pool with five porticoes (porches). The bread and fish remind us of the miracle of the multiplication of the loaves and fishes. Jesus at the altar with the temple reminds us that Jesus went to the Temple of Jerusalem to preach his message. The woman and the stones reminds us of that dramatic event where Jesus refused to condemn the adulteress, yet commanded her to sin no more. The mirror depicts another glorious miracle in which Jesus gave the blind man sight. This is also a reminder of the sacraments, since Jesus used material things (spittle and clay in this case), to work the healing. Finally, the good shepherd reminds us of Jesus Himself, and how he gave his life for his sheep – those sheep including you and me.

Note also the role of the *numbers* of the locations. In this particular demonstration, they represent the *chapter numbers* within the Gospel of St. John, in which these events are found. This means that *you* now know one major event or lesson within the first ten chapters of the John's Gospel – in order!

You now know well that building a series of locations enhances our power to remember things well, and in their exact order. And indeed, once a series of locations is well learned, like the ten that were just provided, they can be used again and again for brand new sets of material. In that way, you can build up all kinds of cathedrals in your mind, to house all kinds of information relevant to the faith that can guide your daily living.

By adding additional places, you can easily store additional information. With twenty-one locations, for example, you could store a key event from *every* chapter in St. John's Gospel, and then go back and add more of the key events and lessons in each chapter, as you store them in your own head and "write them on the tablet of your heart."

Purchasing Understanding and Love with the Treasures We Store in Our Memory

I would hope that if you do take the trouble to *memorize* the key events of all the chapters of St. John's Gospel, you would also seek out means to more fully grasp and *understand* their deeper meanings. This can be accomplished by prayerful meditation upon the text and through the thoughtful readings of trustworthy commentaries. As Catholics, we are blessed with nearly two millennia full of devout and learned saints, Church Fathers, and Doctors who have commented on this gospel. Among the greatest commentaries is that of the Angelic Doctor, St. Thomas Aquinas himself. His *Commentary of the Gospel of St. John,* as we noted, devotes about 65 pages to the fourteen verses of the Last Gospel alone. The whole commentary, in two volumes in the Latin/English edition I use, weighs in at a total of one-thousand and seven pages! Further, the reason his commentary is so magnificent and glorious is that he incorporates the insights of dozens of Greek and Latin Church Fathers and Doctors who preceded him.

So, for those who may have enjoyed exercising their powers of memory on key themes from the first ten chapters St. John using the memory methods of Sts. Albert the Great and Thomas Aquinas, *we invite you to look* for *a forthcoming series of books that will help you and your families remember the key events and lessons of the life of Christ in every single chapter of all four gospels.* The first in the series will be entitled *Memorize John! (And Contemplate Christ!) A Thomistic Guide to the Gospel of St. John.*

The memory method itself will *not* use a house or a church, but will employ a very simple and effective location system not used in print, to our knowledge, in over 500 years![8] More important still, the commentary on each chapter will borrow most heavily from the insights of the Angelic Doctor himself. In this way, through our best efforts, and God's most generous grace, we will seek to use the treasures of truth stored in our memories to purchase deeper understanding and deeper love of He Who as St. John's Gospel makes clear for us "was with God…was God," (1:1) and is "the way, the truth, and the life." (14:6).

May God bless you and yours until we meet again --- at the Gospel of St. John!

---

8 (Hint: See Ezekiel 1:5-11 and Revelation [Apocalypse] 4:6-8).

Made in United States
Orlando, FL
06 July 2022